DATE DU

The Theory and Practice of Nonpar Banking

The Theory
and Practice
of Nonpar Banking

PAUL F. JESSUP

Northwestern University Press
Evanston   1967

PAUL F. JESSUP is Visiting Assistant Professor
of Finance in the School of Business at
Northwestern University.

Preface

Many individuals and institutions contributed to the preparation of this study. Much of the information was developed from interviews with bankers and bank supervisory authorities. Of major importance were extensive interviews with nonpar bankers and par bankers in Georgia and Minnesota. In all cases these gentlemen were generous with their time and thoughtful in their replies to my questions concerning various features of nonpar banking.

Recognizing my indebtedness to many people, I should like to acknowledge the specific assistance of four individuals. Mr. Raymond E. Hengren, of the Federal Deposit Insurance Corporation, first suggested the topic for my consideration, and he facilitated my efforts to accomplish the necessary research rapidly and comprehensively. By suggesting procedures and by providing me with computer time, Mr. Lee W. Langham, Assistant Director, Division of Data Processing of the Board of Governors of the Federal Reserve System, expedited my data collection and calculation. Mrs. Mary Mitchell, of the Federal Deposit Insurance Corporation, provided important guidance in the selection and use of appropriate statistical techniques. Professor Donald P. Jacobs, chairman of my dissertation committee at Northwestern University, provided thoughtful encouragement and advice on this research project and throughout my graduate studies.

In various ways I received research assistance from the Federal Deposit Insurance Corporation, the American Bankers Association, and the Board of Governors of the Federal Reserve System. Although these institutions provided aggregate data for my analysis, they have

v

in no way endorsed my interpretation of the data or my policy conclusions.

During the academic year 1965–66, while conducting my research and analysis, I was the recipient of a Stonier Fellowship in Banking.

Publication of this study is being sponsored by the Federal Reserve Bank of Minneapolis to facilitate broader understanding and discussion of the issues of nonpar banking. The role of the Federal Reserve Bank of Minneapolis has been limited, as the study was completed before it came to the Bank's attention.

Responsibility for the information, analysis, and conclusions in this study rests with the author.

PAUL F. JESSUP

Table of Contents

LIST OF TABLES   xi

I
INTRODUCTION   3

II
THE HISTORICAL BACKGROUND OF NONPAR BANKING   6
The Origins of the Clearing and Collection System of the Federal
    Reserve Banks
Attempts by the Federal Reserve Banks to Achieve Universal Par
    Clearance
Opposition to Measures Used by the Federal Reserve Banks in
    Their Attempts to Achieve Universal Par Clearance
In Summary

III
A SURVEY OF NONPAR BANKING: 1940–64   14
The Absorption-of-Exchange Controversy
State Legislation Prohibiting Nonpar Banking
Recent Statements concerning Nonpar Banking
The Need for Further Analysis

IV
THE CURRENT STRUCTURE OF NONPAR BANKING   23
Certain Characteristics of Nonpar Banks
Ownership of Nonpar Banks
Nonpar Branches

Table of Contents

V

AN ANALYSIS OF CERTAIN OPERATING CHARACTERISTICS OF NONPAR
   BANKS   30
Selection of Similar Groups of Banks for Comparative Purposes
Description of Operating Ratios Used to Measure Comparative
   Operating Characteristics
Comparison of Operating Performance within Each of Eight
   States
Evaluation of Operating Ratios for Nonpar Banks in Rural One-
   Bank Towns in Six States
Comparison of Operating Characteristics of Aggregate Nonpar
   Banks Classified by Various Structures of Competition
Conclusions

VI

THE IMPORTANCE OF EXCHANGE INCOME TO NONPAR BANKS   47
Current Maximum Contribution of Exchange Income to Total
   Operating Revenue of Various Nonpar Banks
Changes in the Maximum Contribution of Exchange Income to
   Total Operating Revenue of Nonpar Banks: 1942–64
Maximum Exchange Income of All Nonpar Banks
Estimated Exchange Income of All Nonpar Banks

VII

CHANGES IN NONPAR BANKS: 1960–64   57
Factors Reducing the Number of Nonpar Banks
Factors Increasing the Number of Nonpar Banks
Summary of Changes

VIII

A CASE STUDY OF CERTAIN BANKS CHANGING FROM NONPAR TO PAR: 67
   1962–63
Selection of a Sample Group of Banks
Findings of the Case Study
Implications of the Case Study

IX

SOME ECONOMIC CONSEQUENCES OF NONPAR BANKING   73
Nonpar Bank Practices and Customers
The Extent of Absorption of Exchange Charges
Why Some Nonpar Banks Become Par: A General Explanation
The Broad Impact of Nonpar Banking

A Model Nonpar Bank Benefiting from Exchange Charges
Summary

X

THE COST BURDEN OF NONPAR BANKING   89
Nonpar Banking Necessarily Imposes Additional Costs on the
    Banking System
Results of a Special Survey Used to Measure the Cost Burden of
    Nonpar Banking
Economies of Scale in Processing Nonpar Checks

XI

CONCLUSIONS   101

STATISTICAL APPENDIX   105

APPENDIX   114

BIBLIOGRAPHY   117

INDEX   121

List of Tables

1 Nonpar banks in nonpar states, classified by number of banks and by total deposits (December 31, 1964)   24

2 A comparison of nonpar and par nonmember banks in nonpar states, classified by location and by structure of local competition (December 31, 1964)   26

3 State bank affiliates of three bank holding companies, classified by par status and by structure of local competition (December 31, 1964)   27

4 Branches of nonpar banks in North Carolina, classified by par status and by structure of local competition (December 31, 1964)   28

5 Branches of par banks that operate some nonpar branches, classified by par status and by structure of local competition (December 31, 1964)   29

6 Number of nonpar and par nonmember banks in rural one-bank towns in nonpar states (December 31, 1964)   31

7 Nonpar and par nonmember banks in rural one-bank towns in eight nonpar states, classified by deposit size (December 31, 1964)   32

List of Tables

8 Summary of this study's analysis of comparative operating characteristics of nonpar and par nonmember banks (December 31, 1964)   33

9 Mean operating ratios of similar nonpar and par nonmember banks in eight nonpar states (1964)   36

10 Nonmember banks in nonpar states reporting *no* revenue from service charges on deposit accounts, classified by structure of local competition (1964)   39

11 Mean operating ratios of nonpar banks in rural one-bank towns in six states (1964)   40

12 Mean operating ratios of nonpar and par banks in fourteen nonpar states, classified by structure of local competition (1964)   42

13 Revenue from "other service charges, commissions, fees, and collection and exchange charges" as a percentage of "total current operating revenue" of nonpar banks, classified by state and by deposit size (1964)   48

14 Revenue from "other service charges, commissions, fees, and collection and exchange charges" as a percentage of "total current operating revenue" of nonpar banks, classified by deposit size and by the years 1942 and 1964   50

15 Total income reported in item 1(e), "other service charges, commissions, fees, and collection and exchange charges," by all nonpar banks, classified by state (1964)   51

16 Exchange charges as a percentage of item 1(e), "other service charges, commissions, fees, and collection and exchange charges," of nonpar banks, classified by the nonpar states included in the "Survey of Par Clearance" (1965)   54

17 Estimate of total income from exchange charges received by all nonpar banks, classified by state (1964)   55

18 Total changes in nonpar banks and nonpar branches, classified by predominant banking structure (1960–64)   57

19 Changes in nonpar banks, classified by factors contributing to change and by predominant banking structure (1960–64)   58

20 New state banks in nonpar states, classified by class of bank and by state (1960–64)   63

21 New insured state banks in selected nonpar states, classified by par status and by structure of local competition (1960–64)   64

22 Banks changing from nonpar to par, classified by structure of local competition (1962–63)   67

23 Mean operating ratios of certain banks that changed from nonpar to par during 1962–63 and a control group of 409 similar banks that remained nonpar (1961, 1964)   70

24 Policies of nonmember banks in ten nonpar states concerning collection of exchange charges on nonpar items deposited by customers (1966)   77

25 Policies of nonmember banks in five nonpar states concerning absorption of exchange charges (1966)   80

26 Mean operating ratios of eight nonpar banks in metropolitan one-bank towns in Minnesota (1964)   87

27 Location by state of the 37 largest banks in the United States, as measured by deposits on December 31, 1965   95

28 Additional cost per item of processing nonpar checks, classified by number of nonpar items processed (figures in cents)   98

The Theory and Practice
of Nonpar Banking

I

Introduction

Most checks in the United States circulate at par. A person receiving a par check usually deposits this item in his bank account and receives full credit for the face amount of the check.

By contrast, a person receiving a check drawn on a nonpar bank and depositing this item in his bank account often does not receive full credit for the face amount of the check. He may deposit the nonpar check in the bank against which the check is drawn (the nonpar bank), but unless he happens to be a resident of the area in which the nonpar bank is located, he is more likely to deposit it in another bank. When this bank sends the check to the nonpar bank for payment, the nonpar bank charges a fee—generally called an "exchange charge"—for paying the check. Typically this charge is one-tenth of 1 per cent, with a minimum of ten cents. For example, a person who receives a nonpar check for $25.00 may find that he eventually receives credit for $24.90. However, if both the writer of the check and the recipient of the check have accounts at the same nonpar bank, there is no exchange charge on the transaction. Both in theory and in practice, exchange charges are made against recipients of checks who live outside the community or general trade area in which a nonpar bank is located.

As of December 31, 1965, there were 1,492 nonpar banks in the United States,[1] accounting for approximately 10 per cent of the total number of banks in the country. However, because nonpar banks are typically small, they accounted for less than 2 per cent of total bank deposits in the United States.

1. *Federal Reserve Bulletin,* LII (February 1966), 273.

The nonpar practice of charging exchange has had a long and controversial history. For many years the issue has been debated in the banking industry, legislatures, courts, and academic circles. The National Monetary Commission, established by Congress in 1908 to study the nation's monetary system, investigated the practice and general implications of nonpar banking. For more than fifty years the Federal Reserve System has sought to implement a policy whereby all checks in the United States would circulate at par. The issue has been widely discussed, and much controversy has been generated—but little analysis. Instead, both critics and proponents of nonpar banking have often relied on general arguments and occasionally on emotional appeals.

The purpose of this study is to present a comprehensive and objective analysis of nonpar banking. Using quantitative methods, it examines how nonpar banks differ from par banks and estimates the importance of exchange income for nonpar banks. Also, by analyzing the practice of nonpar banking in the context of the nation's banking system, it measures the impact of that practice both on other banks and on individuals. Most of the statistical information used in this study has been prepared and presented for the first time.

Chapters II and III contain a brief history of nonpar banking from 1900 through 1964 in order to supply the necessary background for a better understanding of the present theory and practice of nonpar banking.

Chapter IV discusses certain characteristics of nonpar banks and the communities they serve—for example, deposit size, ownership, and the competitive environment in which nonpar banks operate.

Chapters V and VI are concerned with certain operating features of nonpar banks and consider two important questions: (1) How do nonpar banks differ from similar par banks in such operating characteristics as profitability, sources of revenue, and asset structure? (2) How important is the revenue from exchange charges to nonpar banks, and has this importance changed through time?

Chapters VII and VIII examine and analyze changes in nonpar banks during the five-year period 1960–64, when the aggregate number of insured nonpar banks decreased by 111, considering also the question of *why* banks change. This analysis is further developed through a case study of certain banks that changed from nonpar to par in the years 1962–63, with emphasis on measures of profitability, sources of revenue, and asset structure *before* and *after* the change.

Chapter IX discusses some important economic consequences of nonpar banking, drawing on the findings presented in preceding chapters and relating them to additional considerations of nonpar policies and their broad and diverse effects.

Chapter X deals with nonpar banking in the context of the nation's banking system, establishing a conceptual framework to analyze the additional costs incurred by par banks in processing nonpar items. Information from a special survey is used to develop a quantified estimate of these costs to one group of banks; the costs are then related to the benefits to the nonpar banks. This analytical framework provides a basis by which one may objectively evaluate the economic efficiency and equity of the practice of charging exchange.

The conclusions of the study are presented in Chapter XI. Here the findings and analyses of the preceding chapters are integrated and expanded to provide conclusions that should be of interest to scholars, bankers, and bank supervisory authorities.

II

The Historical Background
of Nonpar Banking

The concept of nonpar banking is deeply rooted in the American banking system. Before the establishment of modern systems of central banking and correspondent banking, transactions among distant banks were at times settled by shipments of gold or currency. The physical transfer of such means of settlement involved a cost, and a principal reason for nonpar banking centered on the question of who should pay that cost.

It was accepted in common law that a check drawn on a bank must be honored at face value when presented for cash or deposit at the same bank.[1] Suppose, however, that a customer of a bank sent a check to a distant city. The recipient of the check deposited it in his bank, and that bank sent the check for collection to the bank against which it was drawn (the drawee bank). If the drawee bank had to send gold or currency to settle the check, a cost was involved. Certain banks asserted that the recipient of the check should pay this cost because the requested transfer of funds to a distant point was a service being performed for him. The recipient's alternative was to pay the cost of having the check presented directly to the bank for full payment. Therefore some banks charged the distant recipient of a check a *remittance charge* for the cost of sending him gold or currency in settlement. This remittance charge usually took the form of a deduction from the face amount of the check. Thus checks sent to distant points were usually honored at less than their face amount by some banks, and the banks following this practice were called *nonpar banks.*

Settlement of checks among various distant banks did not always

1. George B. Vest, "The Par Collection System of the Federal Reserve Banks," *Federal Reserve Bulletin,* XXVI (February 1940), 89.

require the physical transfer of gold or currency. Often banks and individuals with balances in money centers would sell part of their balances in the form of *exchange drafts*. If a check were sent for collection to a drawee bank from a distant money center, the drawee bank could make settlement by buying an exchange draft in that money center. Charges for such exchange drafts varied, reflecting changes in the supply of and demand for funds in different money centers, but the purchase of a draft was often more practical and less expensive than the physical transfer of funds. Nonpar banks asserted that the cost of an exchange draft should be borne by the distant recipient of the check because the service was being performed for him. Therefore they usually deducted an *exchange charge* from the face amount of checks sent from distant points for collection.

In practice the terms *remittance charge* and *exchange charge* were synonymous. Both were related to the concept that the cost of tranferring settlement funds to a distant point should be borne by the recipient of a check requiring a transfer of funds. This transfer cost was customarily deducted from the face amount of the check as an exchange (remittance) charge. Because such checks were honored at less than face value, banks following this procedure were called nonpar banks.

THE ORIGINS OF THE CLEARING AND COLLECTION SYSTEM

OF THE FEDERAL RESERVE BANKS

The panic of 1907, with its suspension of gold payments and the attendant failure of many banks, resulted in discussion and criticism of the nation's monetary system. In response to such criticism, Congress established in 1908 a National Monetary Commission, consisting of nine senators and nine representatives, to study the nation's monetary system and recommend improvements.[2] The commission authorized extensive research in the areas of money and banking and made detailed studies of monetary policies and practices in the United States and other countries.

In its studies the National Monetary Commission observed various deficiencies in the nation's monetary system. Among these were (1) the inefficient process of clearing checks through correspondent banks, (2) the high exchange charges, and (3) the circuitous routing of

2. Raymond P. Kent, *Money and Banking* (New York, 1966), p. 401.

7

checks.[3] This third deficiency refers to the fact that a nonpar bank at times agreed to honor its checks at par if such checks were sent to it by a certain correspondent bank.[4] Learning of such an agreement, other banks that received checks drawn on the nonpar bank frequently sent these checks to the correspondent bank which could clear them at par. This circuitous routing of checks to avoid exchange charges usually prolonged the clearing time and increased the handling costs.

These studies and proposals for reform of the nation's monetary system contributed to the passage of the Federal Reserve Act in 1913. Among its diverse objectives this act provided for the establishment of check-clearing facilities through the Federal Reserve banks.

Unfortunately the Federal Reserve Act was ambiguous concerning par clearance and exchange charges. Two sentences from Section 16 reflect this ambiguity:

> Every Federal reserve bank shall receive on deposit *at par* from member banks or from Federal reserve banks checks and drafts drawn upon any of its depositors, and when remitted by a Federal reserve bank, checks and drafts drawn by any depositor in any other Federal reserve bank upon funds to the credit of said depositor in said reserve bank or member bank. Nothing herein contained shall be construed as prohibiting a member bank from *charging its actual expense incurred in collecting and remitting funds,* or for *exchange* sold to its patrons.[5] [Italics added.]

The language of this section of the act seemed to establish par clearance as a goal of check clearance, particularly within the Federal Reserve System; yet it recognized and apparently authorized certain features of exchange charges. This apparent inconsistency—particularly in practice—contributed to varying interpretations, controversial policies, and extensive litigation.

While the act was imprecise concerning par clearance, it did authorize broad administrative flexibility for the Federal Reserve Board. The power of the board to issue rulings concerning check-clearing procedures was defined in Section 16:

> The Federal Reserve Board shall make and promulgate from time to time regulations governing the transfer of funds and charges therefor among Federal reserve banks and their branches, and may at its discretion exercise the functions of a clearing house for such Federal reserve banks, or may

3. "Nonpar Banking: Near the End of an Era?" *Monthly Review* (Federal Reserve Bank of Minneapolis), May 1966, p. 5.
4. Vest, p. 90.
5. *First Annual Report of the Federal Reserve Board for the Period Ending December 31, 1914* (Washington, 1915), p. 135.

8

designate a Federal reserve bank to exercise such functions, and may also require each such bank to exercise the functions of a clearing house for its member banks.[6]

Given such broad powers, the Federal Reserve Board was able to develop regulations that might implement its policies concerning the clearing of checks at par.

ATTEMPTS BY THE FEDERAL RESERVE BANKS TO ACHIEVE

UNIVERSAL PAR CLEARANCE

Based on the provisions of the Federal Reserve Act, a check-clearing system was adopted by the Federal Reserve banks in 1915. From June 1915 to July 1916 this clearing system was voluntary, but less than 25 per cent of the eligible banks participated in it.[7] A principal reason for their reluctance to participate was the concern that they would be forced to relinquish their income from exchange charges.

Because of the lack of response to the voluntary system, in 1916 the Federal Reserve Board issued Regulation J, whereby member banks were required to remit at par on all checks presented to them by the Federal Reserve banks.[8] The effectiveness of this compulsory procedure was limited because the Federal Reserve banks were authorized to collect only checks drawn on member banks and deposited by a member bank or another Federal Reserve bank.[9] Also this compulsory system was opposed by some member banks because they were required to honor their checks at par while nonmember banks could still levy exchange charges.

In view of the limited effectiveness of the initial compulsory system and the internal opposition to it, the Federal Reserve Act was amended to broaden the classes of checks that Federal Reserve banks could clear for their members.[10] Federal Reserve banks were authorized to accept for collection checks drawn on nonmember banks in

6. *Ibid.*

7. *Second Annual Report of the Federal Reserve Board for the Year Ending December 31, 1915* (Washington, 1916), p. 16.

8. *Third Annual Report of the Federal Reserve Board Covering Operations for the Year 1916* (Washington, 1917), p. 9.

9. Melvin C. Miller, *The Par Check Collection and Absorption of Exchange Controversies* (Cambridge, Massachusetts, 1949), p. 17.

10. *Fourth Annual Report of the Federal Reserve Board Covering Operations for the Year 1917* (Washington, 1918), p. 23.

their respective districts. Given this authority, the Federal Reserve Board ruled that Federal Reserve banks could receive for collection only checks drawn on those nonmember banks that would remit at par to the Federal Reserve banks.[11] The broadened legal authority and attendant administrative ruling did not bring many nonmember banks into the check-clearing system of the Federal Reserve banks, nor did they provide much incentive for nonmember banks to agree to honor their checks at par.

The continuing controversy concerning par clearance and exchange charges was reflected in congressional debate, presidential correspondence, an amendment to the Federal Reserve Act, and a written opinion by the Attorney General of the United States. Despite attempts to settle the controversy, it continued to be vigorous—and unresolved.

Confronted by the unwillingness of many nonmember banks to remit at par, the Federal Reserve Board acted to enforce par clearance. As interpreted by the Board, the Federal Reserve Act obligated it to establish a system of universal par clearance. To achieve this objective, the Board turned to the provision of common law whereby banks had to honor at par those checks drawn on them and presented over the counter. With the approval of the Federal Reserve Board, several Federal Reserve banks began to accumulate checks drawn on nonpar banks in their districts and arranged to have the checks presented at the counters of these nonpar banks.[12] To achieve this direct presentation, the Federal Reserve banks used their own officials or employed agents located in communities with nonpar banks. Although such procedures were costly and resulted in intensified opposition to the Federal Reserve System, the board justified them by its interpretation of its responsibilities under the Federal Reserve Act.

At first the Federal Reserve Board had published a "par list," which contained the names of only those nonmember banks that had agreed to remit at par to the Federal Reserve banks. Under the new policy of presenting checks over the counter, the par list expanded rapidly because it began to include names of banks from which Federal Reserve banks were collecting at par by presenting checks over the counter. This procedure resulted in spurious figures concerning the extent of par banking at the time. Many banks on the par list had not consented to being placed on it, considered themselves to be nonpar banks, and strongly opposed the tactics of the Federal Reserve System.

11. *Ibid.*, p. 181.
12. Walter Earl Spahr, *The Clearing and Collection of Checks* (New York, 1926), p. 245.

OPPOSITION TO MEASURES USED BY THE FEDERAL

RESERVE BANKS IN THEIR ATTEMPTS TO ACHIEVE

UNIVERSAL PAR CLEARANCE

As time progressed, opposition to the policy of imposing par clearance on all banks became intensified and more organized. Obstructive tactics were adopted by many nonpar banks to discourage agents of the Federal Reserve System from presenting checks over the counter. Often an agent would be subjected to delays at the counter, or would be paid in small coins, which were cumbersome to transport. Or he might be paid by exchange draft, thus delaying the final receipt of funds by the Federal Reserve banks. In view of such hostility on the part of nonpar banks, the Federal Reserve banks found it increasingly difficult to recruit local agents to present checks to nonpar banks.

To form a strong and united opposition to the imposition of par clearance, the National and State Bankers Protective Association was organized in 1920. This association, principally representing country bankers, was reported to have a membership of 15,000 banks in that same year.[13] Its objective was to promote state laws recognizing the right of state banks to charge exchange and protecting these banks from coercion by the Federal Reserve banks. In addition, the association proposed to present the case for nonpar banking before the United States Congress.

The legislatures of some states did pass laws favorable to nonpar banking, among them Alabama, Florida, Georgia, Louisiana, Mississippi, North Carolina, South Dakota, and Tennessee. In general these laws stipulated that banks in the state, both state and national, should make exchange charges as fixed by custom on checks presented for payment by or through any bank, trust company, Federal Reserve bank, express company, or any other agency.[14] The maximum rate for exchange charges was fixed, usually at one-eighth or one-tenth of 1 per cent of the face amount of the check. Claiming that such laws were unconstitutional when they required national banks and state member banks to charge exchange, the Federal Reserve banks generally continued their attempts to enforce par clearance.

The more organized opposition and the enactment of state laws favoring nonpar banking shifted the controversy to the courts. At

13. Miller, p. 25.
14. *Ibid.*, p. 26.

times litigation related to nonpar banking was carried to the Supreme Court of the United States. From these cases concerning the clearing and collection procedures of the Federal Reserve System, certain principles were established and have been summarized as follows:

1. The Federal Reserve Act so far as it affects the clearing and collection system is not mandatory in nature and does not compel the Federal Reserve Board or Federal reserve banks to make the system universal.

2. Federal reserve banks are not obliged to receive and attempt to collect checks drawn on banks which will not remit at par.

3. Federal reserve banks *may* receive and attempt to collect checks on banks which will not remit at par by presenting the checks directly over the counters of such banks through the use of collecting agents, provided the Federal reserve banks do not use this method to oppress or coerce, by collecting an unusual amount of checks for presentation or by indulging in other practice not consistent with customary banking methods.

4. So far as the non-member banks are concerned the Federal reserve clearing and collection system is entirely voluntary.

5. Federal reserve banks may not include on their par lists the names of non-member banks which do not agree voluntarily to remit at par and do not sanction the publication of their names. All member banks, obviously, are par banks.

6. Federal reserve banks cannot lawfully demand payment in legal tender if a State law, which supersedes the common law, permits the non-member banks to make arrangements with their depositors to remit in some other form, since the debt of the bank has been held to be solely to the depositor of the bank and not to the holder of the check, and if the depositor and drawer of the check consents to have the bank pay the holders of his checks by some means other than legal tender, the legal tender provisions of the Constitution which prohibit a State from making anything but gold and silver coin a tender in payments, are not violated.[15]

In view of the court decisions, the continued opposition to their tactics, and the heavy expenses involved in presenting checks over the counter to recalcitrant banks, in 1923 the Federal Reserve banks retreated, refraining from further direct efforts to enforce par clearance for all banks. Nevertheless the Federal Reserve System continued to adhere to the goal of universal par clearance and sought to achieve it indirectly through subsequent rulings and legislative recommendations (Chapter III).

IN SUMMARY

Historically in the United States, exchange charges were extensively used and generally accepted. In January 1918 more than 11,300 banks

15. Spahr, pp. 288–89.

were not on the par list, while about 9,300 nonmember banks were on the list.[16] As shown in Table A–1 of the Statistical Appendix, in August 1919 there were nonpar banks in 35 states.

The Federal Reserve System, considering itself obligated to establish universal par clearance, adopted strong, controversial measures to achieve this objective. Its confidence in its ability to do so is illustrated by an assertion by the Federal Reserve Board in 1917: "It is believed that in the near future checks upon practically all banks in the United States can be collected at par by Federal Reserve Banks." [17] The attempt of the Federal Reserve System to impose par remittance on all banks was increasingly met by organized opposition. Various state legislatures passed laws favorable to nonpar banking, and some of these laws remain valid.

Because of the intensity of the par collection controversy, a legacy of suspicion and even bitterness continued to exist for many years. Many nonpar bankers, in opposing the attempts of the Federal Reserve System to impose universal par clearance, apparently visualized themselves as upholding states' rights and championing the rights of the small man. Although it retreated from its measures to enforce par remittance by nonmember banks, the Federal Reserve System never abandoned its goal of universal par clearance.

16. *Ibid.*, p. 247.
17. *Third Annual Report of the Federal Reserve Board Covering Operations for the Year 1916*, p. 10.

III
A Survey of Nonpar Banking: 1940–64

At year-end 1939 there were 2,656 nonpar banks in the United States, accounting for 18 per cent of all commercial banks at the time [1] and reflecting a major decrease from the 11,336 nonpar banks reported on January 15, 1918—approximately 20 years earlier.[2]

One reason for the sharp decline in the number of nonpar banks was the Federal Reserve System's continued effort to achieve a nationwide system of par clearance. After retreating from its attempts to compel nonmember banks to remit at par, the Federal Reserve System sought to achieve its goal by indirect methods, such as encouraging state banks to join the system and persuading nonmember banks to remit at par to Federal Reserve banks. While trying to increase its membership, however, the Federal Reserve System was constantly confronted by the problem of withdrawals. The reason given by some withdrawing banks was their desire to increase their revenue by making exchange charges.[3]

The Banking Acts of 1933 and 1935 provided the Federal Reserve System with new powers by which the goal of universal par clearance might be indirectly achieved.

THE ABSORPTION-OF-EXCHANGE CONTROVERSY

In theory the distant recipient of a nonpar check pays the exchange charge because he is the person requiring additional service—the

1. George B. Vest, "The Par Collection System of the Federal Reserve Banks," *Federal Reserve Bulletin*, XXVI (February 1940), 94. This figure excludes 65 private banks not under state supervision.
2. Walter Earl Spahr, *The Clearing and Collection of Checks* (New York, 1926), p. 247.
3. Vest, p. 95.

transfer of settlement funds to him. At times, however, the bank at which he deposits the check may credit him with its face amount and pay the exchange charge itself, thus incurring an operating expense. This practice, whereby a bank pays exchange charges for its customers, is known as *absorption of exchange charges.*

A bank may absorb exchange charges for various reasons. If the number of nonpar items presented to a bank is few and the applicable exchange charges are small, the bank may decide that absorbing the exchange charges costs less than passing them back to their recipients. Then, too, a bank may adopt such a policy to avoid irritating its customers. Or it may actively absorb exchange charges as a service to solicit new customers, specifically corporations or correspondent banks. In providing this service the bank generally requires the customer to maintain an adequate balance, the value of which will compensate the bank for its absorption of exchange charges (Chapter IX). The practice of aggressively offering to absorb exchange charges as a competitive device—particularly to obtain correspondent balances—became the center of the *absorption-of-exchange controversy.*

Included in the Banking Act of 1933 was a provision that prohibited banks which were members of the Federal Reserve System from paying interest on demand deposits, "directly or indirectly by any device whatsoever."[4] While prohibiting such payment of interest on demand deposits by *member* banks, the act did not define the term "interest," nor did it give power to the Board of Governors to define the term. This lack of a precise definition resulted in varying interpretations and accompanying controversies.

In an attempt to resolve the issue, the Banking Act of 1935 gave power to the Board of Governors to define the term "interest" under this law and to issue regulations to enforce such prohibition of interest on demand deposits by member banks.[5] Given this power of definition and regulation, the Board of Governors defined the payment of interest on demand deposits as including the absorption of exchange charges when this resulted in out-of-pocket expenses for member banks. A revised regulation, based on that definition, was to become effective on January 1, 1936.[6]

The Banking Act of 1935 also required the Federal Deposit Insurance Corporation to prohibit *insured nonmember* banks from paying

---

4. *Federal Reserve Bulletin,* XIX (June 1933), 394.
5. *Ibid.,* XXI (December 1935), 793.
6. *Ibid.*

interest on demand deposits.[7] However, although the act gave the Board of Governors the power to define "interest," it gave the Federal Deposit Insurance Corporation only the authority to define *demand deposits*. Thus, because of its interpretation of the meaning of the act and its authority under the act, the Federal Deposit Insurance Corporation did not rule that the absorption of exchange charges by insured nonmember banks was payment of interest on demand deposits.

In view of the position adopted by the Federal Deposit Insurance Corporation, the Board of Governors deferred the effective date of its proposed regulation prohibiting member banks from absorbing exchange charges. It was hoped that the two bank supervisory agencies would be able to adopt a similar regulation concerning absorption of exchange charges.

The question whether absorption of exchange charges was or was not an indirect payment of interest remained dormant until September 1943. At that time the Board of Governors ruled that absorption of exchange charges by a particular member bank constituted a payment of interest on demand deposits and therefore violated Section 19 of the Federal Reserve Act and the Board's Regulation Q.[8] This ruling concerning a particular member bank was extended to prohibit absorption of exchange by any member bank.

Although the Board of Governors stated that it issued this regulation only to carry out its responsibilities under the Banking Act of 1935, it seems evident that the board also regarded this procedure as an indirect stimulus toward par banking.[9] Prohibiting member banks from absorbing exchange charges meant that such charges would have to be passed on to recipients of nonpar checks. These recipients, directly confronted with the cost of exchange charges, might complain to depositors in nonpar banks, who in turn might put pressure on their banks to remit at par.

Shortly after this ruling by the Board of Governors, the Federal Deposit Insurance Corporation reasserted its position that absorption of exchange charges by nonmember banks was *not* to be considered as payment of interest, "in the absence of facts or circumstances es-

7. Walter Wyatt, "The Par Clearance Controversy," *Virginia Law Review*, XXX (June 1944), 363.
8. *Federal Reserve Bulletin*, XXIX (September 1943), 817–18.
9. U. S. Congress, House Committee on Banking and Currency, *Hearings on H.R.3956, Absorption of Exchange Charges*, 78th Cong., 2d Sess., 1943–44, p. 599. Cited hereafter as *Hearings, Absorption of Exchange Charges*.

tablishing that the practice is resorted to as a device for payment of interest." [10]

Each agency justified its position by its interpretation of statutory authority. The Board of Governors maintained that absorption of exchange charges was clearly an indirect payment of interest on demand deposits, a practice that the board was obligated and empowered to prohibit under the terms of the Banking Act of 1935. The Federal Deposit Insurance Corporation maintained that historically the practice of absorbing exchange charges had never been considered to be payment of interest and that, lacking the power to define "interest," the corporation could not prohibit this practice any more than it could prohibit other "free" banking services commonly provided to customers with demand deposits.[11]

Because the two banking agencies had adopted opposing positions on the issue of absorbing exchange charges, intense controversy developed in banking and government circles. One result of that controversy was an extended series of congressional hearings on the subject of absorption of exchange charges.[12] These hearings recorded diverse testimony on the issues of nonpar banking and absorption of exchange charges. At the same time a special study was prepared by the Federal Deposit Insurance Corporation. This study, appended to the hearings, was principally a comparison of par and nonpar banks in 27 nonpar states in 1942,[13] but it also attempted to analyze the probable effect on nonpar banks of a loss of revenue from exchange charges. On the basis of this analysis the Federal Deposit Insurance Corporation concluded that "loss of 'remittance exchange' would impose adjustments which many nonpar banks would find difficult, if not impossible, to make." [14]

This study of nonpar banking was important for several reasons: (1) It was one of very few attempts to analyze the subject of nonpar banking by using quantitative data. While the analysis was limited in scope, it was an important exception to the customary general arguments about nonpar banking. (2) Its methodology provided a model for comparing and improving subsequent methods of analysis. (3) Its data supplied a useful bench mark for subsequent comparisons. (4) The study seems to have posed the right questions and tried to answer

10. *Ibid.*, p. 603.
11. *Ibid.*, p. 599.
12. *Ibid.*, pp. 1–752.
13. *Ibid.*, pp. 713–36.
14. *Ibid.*, p. 719.

these questions—one conclusion being that many nonpar banks at the time might not be able to adjust to the loss of income from exchange charges.[15]

Another result of the controversy was the attempt by some congressmen to amend the Federal Reserve Act so that absorption of exchange or collection charges would *not* be prohibited as payment of interest on demand deposits.[16] Such an amendment did pass in the House of Representatives but was defeated when introduced as a rider in the Senate and died with the adjournment of the Seventy-eighth Congress.

While the Board of Governors in theory maintained its basic position prohibiting absorption of exchange charges by member banks, it modified its prohibition in practice. As has been noted, a bank may want to absorb occasional small exchange charges in order to avoid the cost and inconvenience of passing these charges back to its customers. Recognizing this situation, in 1945 the Board of Governors addressed all member banks, stating that absorption of exchange charges "in amounts aggregating not more than $2.00 for any one depositor in any calendar month or in any other regularly established period of 30 days will be considered as trivial and will be disregarded."[17] Member banks that absorbed exchange charges exceeding the authorized amount were presumed to be violating the law prohibiting the payment of interest on demand deposits. This authorization of member banks to absorb limited amounts of exchange charges has become known as the "$2 Rule." Briefly abandoned in 1960 when the Board attempted to prohibit absorption of any exchange charges, the rule was reinstated later the same year.[18]

Currently, with the qualification of the $2 Rule, *member* banks are prohibited from absorbing exchange charges, while *nonmember* banks are free to absorb exchange charges. This situation, in which two classes of commercial banks operate under differing regulations of federal banking agencies, has resulted in further controversy.[19]

15. Some of the analytical procedures used by the Federal Deposit Insurance Corporation to reach this conclusion are evaluated in Chapter VI, which is concerned with measuring the current importance of exchange income for nonpar banks. Also, in Chapter VI some of the data from the 1942 study are used for comparative purposes.

16. *Hearings, Absorption of Exchange Charges*, p. 160.

17. *Federal Reserve Bulletin*, XXXI (June 1945), 564.

18. *Ibid.*, XLVI (November 1960), 1226.

19. U. S. Treasury Department, Comptroller of the Currency, *National Banks and the Future*, Report of the Advisory Committee on Banking to the Comptroller of the Currency (Washington, 1962), p. 125. Cited hereafter as *National Banks and the Future*.

STATE LEGISLATION PROHIBITING NONPAR BANKING

In 1943 Iowa became the first state to pass a law requiring that its state-chartered banks and trust companies should clear their checks at par.[20] Par-clearance laws were subsequently passed in Nebraska (1945) and Wisconsin (1949).[21] In other nonpar states similar par-clearance legislation was proposed but was defeated in legislative committee or on the floor of the legislature.

In some states attempts were made to achieve par clearance by means of voluntary abolition of exchange charges. Michigan and Montana, for example, achieved such voluntary abolition through the state banking associations.[22] A similar attempt to achieve voluntary par clearance in North Dakota was unsuccessful.[23]

RECENT STATEMENTS CONCERNING NONPAR BANKING

The issues of nonpar banking and absorption of exchange charges have been considered in recent studies of the nation's monetary system. Furthermore, some of these studies have adopted positions or made proposals concerning nonpar banking.

The Commission on Money and Credit, in its report published in 1961, observed that "many nonmember banks make an exchange charge in settling checks drawn on them, and this constitutes an imperfection in the payments mechanism." [24] Partly because of this situation but basically because of different reserve requirements among member and nonmember banks, the commission recommended that all insured commercial banks be required to become members of the Federal Reserve System.

In 1962 the Advisory Committee on Banking considered exchange charges in its report to the Comptroller of the Currency. While referring to exchange charges as "an imperfection in our banking system," the report did state that for many small banks such charges

---

20. Iowa, *Iowa Code, Annotated* (1949), c. 528, sec. 63.

21. "Nonpar Banking: Near the End of an Era?" *Monthly Review* (Federal Reserve Bank of Minneapolis), May 1966, p. 6.

22. *Ibid.*

23. Melvin C. Miller, *The Par Check Collection and Absorption of Exchange Controversies* (Cambridge, Massachusetts, 1949), pp. 85–87.

24. The Report of the Commission on Money and Credit, *Money and Credit: Their Influence on Jobs, Prices, and Growth* (Englewood Cliffs, New Jersey, 1961), p. 77.

constituted "an important source of revenue." [25] Moreover, the report saw it as "manifestly inappropriate" that the Federal Reserve System and the Federal Deposit Insurance Corporation should maintain opposing positions concerning absorption of exchange charges, and recommended that legislation should be sought requiring all insured commercial banks to clear their checks at par.

The Committee on Financial Institutions submitted its report to the President of the United States in 1963. The committee regarded the practice of making exchange charges as "an impediment in the payments mechanism of the United States" and as "costly and time consuming" for other banks.[26] After expressing these views, the report stated: "The Committee favors par clearance in principle. But it recognizes that elimination of the impediment in the payments system would materially affect the 1,600 banks (with 1,900 offices) that do not now remit at par." [27] Having stated its general observations, the committee made no recommendations concerning nonpar banking.

Finally, in its Annual Report for 1965 the Board of Governors of the Federal Reserve System expressed the opinion that "there is no sound reason for any bank to pay less than the face amount of checks drawn on it," [28] and recommended enactment of legislation requiring all insured banks to remit at par on their checks. Shortly afterward *The New York Times,* in an editorial titled "Banking Anachronisms," called for congressional prohibition of exchange charges.[29]

The preceding statements by influential committees illustrate the major points made in the continuing debate on nonpar banking. However, another salient fact also emerges: Important statements and recommendations concerning nonpar banking have been based on inadequate analysis. In the first place, opposition to nonpar banking often is based on the argument that the practice is a departure from an "ideal" payments mechanism; this is basically a judgmental argument. Second, the practice of nonpar banking is said to be costly and time consuming for other banks. This is true, but the statement should be carefully defined and quantified. Third, some statements seem to disregard the probable effect on nonpar banks if they should lose their rev-

25. *National Banks and the Future,* p. 125.

26. U. S. Committee on Financial Institutions, *Report of the Committee on Financial Institutions to the President of the United States* (Washington, 1963), p. 9.

27. *Ibid.*

28. *Fifty-second Annual Report of the Board of Governors of the Federal Reserve System, Covering Operations for the Year 1965* (Washington, 1966), p. 240.

29. *The New York Times,* May 3, 1966, p. 46.

enue from exchange charges. Other statements assert that exchange revenue is important to nonpar banks and that elimination of such revenue would materially affect these banks, but no evidence is provided for these assertions, which should be carefully defined and measured.

THE NEED FOR FURTHER ANALYSIS

In the period from 1918 through 1939 the total number of nonpar banks decreased by about 8,700. In a period of comparable length, from 1942 through 1964, the total number of insured nonpar banks decreased by 940.[30] Of these, 360 were in the three states that passed legislation requiring par clearance, 134 were in nine other states in which nonpar banking gradually ended, and 446 were in present nonpar states. This means that over a 22-year period there was a "natural attrition" of only 580 nonpar banks—a decrease of 24 per cent. At such a rate of decrease, the practice of nonpar banking will continue for many years.

Basing its action on the Banking Act of 1935, the Board of Governors ruled that *member* banks were prohibited from absorbing exchange charges (as qualified by the $2 Rule). The Federal Deposit Insurance Corporation did not prohibit *nonmember* banks from absorbing exchange charges. These conflicting positions of the two federal banking agencies have remained unreconciled for over twenty years.

Enforcement of the absorption prohibition burdens member banks with the cost of recording exchange charges and passing them back to their customers. If the Board of Governors believed that prohibiting member banks from absorbing these charges would encourage nonpar banks to begin remitting at par, it is doubtful that its objective has been achieved. The ineffectiveness of this indirect procedure is demonstrated by three facts: (1) The number of nonpar banks has not decreased rapidly—particularly in present nonpar states. (2) Nonmember banks have remained free to absorb exchange charges. (3) Absorption of exchange charges is rare in certain major nonpar states (Chapter IX). The question that must be asked, and cannot readily be answered, is whether nonpar banking would have become *more prevalent* if member banks had been permitted to absorb exchange charges.

30. Special tabulation prepared by the Federal Deposit Insurance Corporation, Washington, 1966.

The practice of nonpar banking, then, has been actively considered in recent general studies of the nation's monetary and banking system. However, statements made in these studies indicate the need for a comprehensive analysis of nonpar banking in the contemporary national economy. Such an analysis would suggest and support specific recommendations concerning nonpar banking.

IV

The Current Structure
of Nonpar Banking

The total number of nonpar banks at the end of 1964 was 1,547.[1] Of these, 1,475 were insured by the Federal Deposit Insurance Corporation and 72 were noninsured. This study is limited to insured nonpar banks because they account for over 95 per cent of all nonpar banks and because of the greater availability of information about them.

The 1,475 insured nonpar banks amounted to about 10 per cent of all insured commercial banks in the United States at year-end 1964, and their total deposits amounted to about 2 per cent of the total deposits in insured commercial banks.[2] While these relationships help place nonpar banking in perspective in the nation's banking system, it is misleading if not erroneous to conclude that the impact of nonpar banking on the nation's economy is insignificant.

Table 1 provides information for measuring the role of nonpar banks in the fifteen states where they operate. Throughout this study these states will be designated "nonpar states." They are located in two principal geographic areas: the upper Middle West (Minnesota, North Dakota, and South Dakota) and the Southeast.

Accounting for about 10 per cent of total insured banks in the United States, the 1,475 nonpar banks account for 27 per cent of all insured banks in the nonpar states; and the range around this average is from less than 1 per cent to 65 per cent. In Georgia, Minnesota, Mississippi, North Dakota, and South Dakota more than 50 per cent of the insured banks are nonpar banks.

1. *Federal Reserve Bulletin*, LI (February 1965), 325.
2. *Annual Report of the Federal Deposit Insurance Corporation, 1964* (Washington, 1965), p. 168.

Table 1. Nonpar banks in nonpar states, classified by number of banks and by total deposits (December 31, 1964)

State	Number of Insured Banks	Number of Insured Nonpar Banks	Per-cent-age	Total Deposits in Insured Banks (millions of dollars)	Deposits in Insured Nonpar Banks (millions of dollars)	Per-cent-age
Alabama	252	76	30	2,843	242	9
Arkansas	241	93	39	1,875	271	14
Florida	421	35	8	6,802	122	2
Georgia	381	218	57	4,025	650	16
Louisiana	208	97	47	3,920	511	13
Minnesota	714	401	56	5,611	1,033	18
Mississippi	194	126	65	1,864	550	30
Missouri	632	45	7	7,992	131	2
North Carolina	151	51	34	4,049	202	5
North Dakota	159	96	60	878	279	32
Oklahoma	416	2	—— *	3,481	3	—— *
South Carolina	129	40	31	1,332	105	8
South Dakota	172	103	60	986	234	24
Tennessee	290	66	23	4,717	194	4
Texas	1,115	26	2	16,632	33	—— *
Total	5,475	1,475	27	67,007	4,560	7

* Less than 0.5 per cent.

Source: Special tabulation prepared by the Federal Deposit Insurance Corporation, 1966.

While the total deposits in the 1,475 nonpar banks are less than 2 per cent of those in insured commercial banks in the United States, the nonpar banks account for 7 per cent of the total deposits in insured banks in the nonpar states; and the range around this average is from less than 1 per cent to 32 per cent. That nonpar banks are generally small is indicated by the fact that the percentage of deposits in nonpar banks is consistently smaller than the percentage of nonpar banks.

The importance of nonpar banking in certain states leads to a consideration of other significant features of nonpar banking: (1) its relationship to bank operating performance, (2) its impact on bank customers and other individuals, and (3) its broader economic implications as measured by the additional costs this practice imposes on other banks in the nation.

CERTAIN CHARACTERISTICS OF NONPAR BANKS

Deposit size. As noted, nonpar banks are generally small institutions. Table A–2 in the Statistical Appendix shows the distribution of insured nonpar banks by state and by deposit size. Forty per cent have total deposits of less than $2,000,000; 45 per cent have total deposits of $2,000,000 to $5,000,000; and 15 per cent have total deposits of $5,000,000 or more. These figures can be seen in perspective when compared with those for all insured commercial banks in the United States. At year-end 1965, 20 per cent had total deposits of less than $2,000,000; 32 per cent had total deposits of $2,000,000 to $5,000,000; and 48 per cent had total deposits of $5,000,000 or more.[3]

Size of communities served. Nonpar banks generally serve small communities, as seen in Table A–3 in the Statistical Appendix, showing the distribution of insured nonpar banks by state and by the population of the communities in which they are located. No less than 50 per cent of the nonpar banks operate in communities of fewer than 1,000 residents, 42 per cent in communities of between 1,000 and 5,000 residents, and only 8 per cent in communities of more than 5,000.

Besides being predominantly small banks in small communities, only 7 per cent of the nonpar banks are located in counties designated as metropolitan areas by the Bureau of the Census. On this basis 93 per cent of the nonpar banks can be classified as rural.

Structure of local competition. Nonpar banks are located predominantly in communities with only one banking facility. Of the 1,473[4] nonpar banks at year-end 1964, 77 per cent were in one-bank towns and 18 per cent in towns with competing nonpar facilities. This phenomenon of two nonpar banks in the same community is most evident in four states—Georgia, Louisiana, Minnesota, and Mississippi—which account for almost 80 per cent of the two-bank cases. Thus while 95 per cent of the nonpar banks are in one-bank towns or towns with a nonpar competitor, only 5 per cent of the nonpar banks are in towns that also have a par banking facility. The preceding figures are taken from Table A–4 in the Statistical Appendix, which shows the distribution of nonpar banks by state, by structure of local competition, and by classification of "rural" and "metropolitan."

These characteristics of nonpar banks are compared with similar

3. *Ibid.,* pp. 202–3.
4. At year-end 1964 there were two insured nonpar banks in Oklahoma. These two banks, which became par institutions in 1965, are omitted from this figure and from the rest of this study.

characteristics of nonmember par banks in the nonpar states in Table 2. Here one observes that nonmember banks which remit at par are frequently located in metropolitan areas. Furthermore they often have a par competitor in the same community, and this par competitor is generally a member of the Federal Reserve System. These findings contrast with the fact that nonpar institutions are predominantly rural banks located in one-bank towns.

Table 2. A comparison of nonpar and par nonmember banks in nonpar states, classified by location and by structure of local competition (December 31, 1964)

	Nonpar		Nonmember Par	
	Number of Banks	Per-centage	Number of Banks	Per-centage
Location in designated geographic area				
Metropolitan *	100	7	585	33
Rural	1,373	93	1,182	67
Structure of local competition				
One-bank town	1,141	77	812	46
Competing nonpar facility in town	258	18	16	1
Competing par facility in town	74	5	939	53
Total	1,473	100	1,767	100

* As designated by the Bureau of the Census.

Source: Special tabulation prepared by the Federal Deposit Insurance Corporation, 1966.

OWNERSHIP OF NONPAR BANKS

From the limited information available, it seems that most nonpar banks are locally owned.

In the upper Middle West three bank holding companies control 26 nonpar banks. In the same nonpar states these three bank holding companies also control 45 state banks that remit at par. Table 3 shows the distribution of these 71 banks by par status and by structure of local competition. Of the 38 affiliates located in one-bank towns or towns where there is a competing nonpar bank, 24 affiliates (63 per cent) are nonpar, while the other 14 affiliates are par. In contrast, of the 33 affiliates located in towns where there is a competing par bank,

Table 3. State bank affiliates of three bank holding companies, classified by par status and by structure of local competition (December 31, 1964) *

Status	Number of Banks, Classified by Structure of Local Competition			
	One-bank Town	Competing Nonpar Bank in Town	Competing Par Bank in Town	Total Banks
Nonpar	13	11	2	26
Par	14	0	31 †	45
Total	27	11	33	71

* First Bank Stock Corporation, Northwest Bancorporation, and Otto Bremer Company.

† Includes five state-member banks of the Federal Reserve System.

Sources: U. S. Congress, House Committee on Banking and Currency, *Bank Holding Companies, Scope of Operations and Stock Ownership*, 88th Cong., 1963, pp. 70–71. *Moody's Bank & Finance Manual* (New York, April 1965), pp. 1060–61, 1153. *Polk's Bank Directory*, March 1965.

only two affiliates are nonpar, while the other 31 affiliates (94 per cent) are par. As one examines the structure of competition confronting nonpar banks, it is evident that the absence or presence of par competition explains much about the structure of, and changes in, nonpar banking.

NONPAR BRANCHES

In states where they are permitted to do so, some nonpar banks operate branches. Branches of nonpar banks are usually nonpar, but at times one finds the phenomenon of a nonpar bank operating some par branches.[5]

North Carolina is the nonpar state having the largest number of nonpar branches, as shown in Table 4, where these branches are classified by par status and by structure of local competition. Of the 20 branches located in one-bank towns, 19 (95 per cent) are nonpar, and only one is par. In contrast, these nonpar banks operate five branches

5. The fact that nonpar banks at times operate par offices was noted by Clifton H. Kreps, Jr., in his article, "Characteristics of Nonpar Banks: A Case Study," *The Southern Economic Journal*, XXVI (July 1959), 47.

Table 4. Branches of nonpar banks in North Carolina, classified by par status and by structure of local competition (December 31, 1964)

| Status | Number of Branches, Classified by Structure of Local Competition | | |
	One-bank Town	Competing Par Facility in Town	Total Branches
Nonpar	19	1	20
Par	1	4	5
Total	20	5	25 *

* Thirteen nonpar banks operate these 25 out-of-town branches and teller windows.

Source: *Polk's Bank Directory*, March 1965.

in towns where there is a competing par facility, and four of these branches are par.

In addition to nonpar banks operating nonpar branches, some banks that are par at their main office operate nonpar branches.[6] This situation is most evident in North Carolina, where nine banks that are par at their main office operated nonpar branches in 65 towns at year-end 1964. The deposit size of these hybrid branch systems ranged from $10,000,000 to $409,000,000 at that time.[7] Table 5 classifies the "par" banks operating nonpar branches in North Carolina and five other states in relation to the structure of local competition. Ninety-seven per cent of the towns in North Carolina where "par" banks operate *nonpar* branches are one-bank towns; 57 per cent of the towns where "par" banks operate *par* branches also have a competing par facility. Similarly in the five other states "par" banks operate 13 nonpar branches and only three par branches in one-bank towns.

A finding that consistently emerges from the preceding analysis is that nonpar banking and branching are principally phenomena of one-bank towns. Only occasionally is a nonpar bank or branch located in a community where it must compete with a par facility.

6. This situation must be recognized in reading the "Federal Reserve Par List," as reported semiannually in the *Federal Reserve Bulletin*. At year-end 1964, 311 nonpar branches and offices were reported (*Federal Reserve Bulletin*, February 1965, p. 325). This figure includes nonpar branches and offices operated by nonpar banks and by banks that are par at their main office.

7. *Polk's Bank Directory* (141st ed.; Nashville, March 1965), North Carolina, pp. 1–57.

Table 5. Branches of par banks that operate some nonpar branches, classified by par status and by structure of local competition (December 31, 1964) *

| | North Carolina | | | | Five Other States † | |
| Structure of Local Competition | Nonpar Branches | | Par Branches | | | |
	Number of Towns	Percentage	Number of Towns	Percentage	Number of Nonpar Branches	Number of Par Branches
One-bank town	63	97	38	43	13	3
Competing nonpar facility in town	——	——	——	——	1	——
Competing par facility in town	2	3	51	57	——	——
Total	65	100	89	100	14	3

* Includes teller windows and paying and receiving stations located outside the head-office community.

† Mississippi, North Dakota, South Carolina, South Dakota, and Tennessee.

Source: *Polk's Bank Directory*, March 1965.

V

An Analysis of Certain Operating Characteristics of Nonpar Banks

SELECTION OF SIMILAR GROUPS OF BANKS

FOR COMPARATIVE PURPOSES

For purposes of analysis it is necessary to compare two groups of banks, nonpar and par, that are as similar in characteristics as possible. All nonpar banks are state banks that are not members of the Federal Reserve System. Therefore they must be compared with par state banks that are likewise not members of the Federal Reserve System. By eliminating member banks one avoids analytical problems related to Federal Reserve membership and its attendant reserve requirements.

Because over 95 per cent of the nonpar banks are insured by the Federal Deposit Insurance Corporation and because data are more readily available for insured banks, this analysis is restricted to *insured* nonmember banks—nonpar and par.

The 1,473 insured nonpar banks at year-end 1964 were located in 14 states, excluding Oklahoma with its two nonpar banks. Therefore the comparison is limited to these 14 states.

Table 2 compares certain characteristics of nonpar and par nonmember banks in nonpar states. It shows, for example, what percentage of each type of bank is located in rural areas: 93 per cent of the nonpar banks as against 67 per cent of the par nonmember banks. Also, one sees that only 5 per cent of the nonpar banks face par competition in the same town, as against 53 per cent of the par nonmember banks. Table A–5 in the Statistical Appendix indicates that nonmember par banks are, on the average, larger in deposit size than nonpar banks in the same states. In view of the wide differences between nonpar and par nonmember banks, it seems desirable to refine further the two groups of banks for comparative purposes.

At year-end 1964, 72 per cent of the insured nonpar banks were located in rural, one-bank towns (Table A–4). Therefore such nonpar banks may well be compared, where possible, with par nonmember banks in rural one-bank towns. The number of these particular nonpar and par nonmember banks in each nonpar state is tabulated in Table

Table 6. Number of nonpar and par nonmember banks in rural one-bank towns in nonpar states (December 31, 1964) *

State	Nonpar	Par
Alabama	50	23
Arkansas	74	25
Florida	27	43
Missouri	42	214
North Carolina	38	13
South Carolina	34	14
Tennessee	47	67
Texas	25	188
Total (eight states)	337 †	587 †
Georgia	114	11
Louisiana	49	4
Minnesota	308	6
Mississippi	70	4
North Dakota	84	3
South Dakota	94	3
Total (six states)	719 †	31
Total (fourteen states)	1,056	618

* In eight states there are sufficient numbers of nonpar and par banks for comparative analysis. In six states there seem to be too few par banks for such analysis.

† These figures exceed those reported in Table A–6, which are lower because of the elimination from this study of banks (1) which were chartered after 1959, (2) which changed from nonpar to par after 1961, and (3) for which there were no data concerning operating ratios.

Source: Special tabulation prepared by the Federal Deposit Insurance Corporation, 1966.

6. It will be noted that in 8 of the 14 nonpar states there seem to be sufficient banks in each classification to justify using them for comparative purposes.

When the two groups of banks are standardized on the basis of location in rural one-bank towns, the deposit-size distributions become very similar, as seen in Table 7. Because of this similarity in

Table 7. Nonpar and par nonmember banks in rural one-bank towns in eight nonpar states, classified by deposit size (December 31, 1964) *

Deposit Size (millions of dollars)	Nonpar		Par	
	Number of Banks	Per-centage	Number of Banks	Per-centage
Under 1	43	13	93	18
1–2	114	34	155	29
2–5	154	46	203	38
5–10	20	6	75	14
10–25	4	1	5	1
Total	335 †	100	531 †	100

* Alabama, Arkansas, Florida, Missouri, North Carolina, South Carolina, Tennessee, and Texas.

† These totals relate to the number of banks used in this comparative study, as outlined in Table A–6.

Source: Special tabulation prepared by the Federal Deposit Insurance Corporation, 1966.

deposit-size distributions and because most of the banks in each group have deposits of under $10,000,000, further stratification by deposit size is neither necessary nor practical.

To have the nonpar and par banks as similar as possible, those banks chartered after 1959 have been removed from each group. Since the majority of such newly chartered banks are par institutions (Chapter VII), to include them might bias the comparison of operating characteristics between the two groups. Also, banks that changed from nonpar to par after 1961 have been excluded from the group of par banks on the assumption that their operating characteristics may be in a period of transition (Chapter VIII).

Given the preceding analytical framework, certain measures of operating performance are compared between nonpar and par banks *within each of eight nonpar states*. Such a comparison, which includes 23 per cent of the nonpar banks, provides statistically valid findings because the two groups of banks are standardized as far as possible.

After the operating performance of nonpar banks in rural one-bank towns has been analyzed, measures of the operating performance of nonpar banks in other competitive environments are examined. Table A–6 in the Statistical Appendix is a complete schematic presentation of this comparative analysis of selected operating characteristics. Certain information from Table A–6 is summarized in Table 8, which shows that 97 per cent of the insured nonpar banks at year-end 1964 are included in the analysis of this comparative study.

Table 8. Summary of this study's analysis of comparative operating characteristics of nonpar and par nonmember banks (December 31, 1964)

	Nonpar		Par
Structure of Local Competition	Number of Banks	Per-centage	Number of Banks
Rural one-bank town			
Eight states	335	23	531
Six states	712	48	——
Competing nonpar bank or branch in town	237	16	——
Competing par bank or branch in town	68	5	——
Metropolitan one-bank town *	79	5	——
Not analyzed	42	3	——
Total	1,473	100	531

* The classification "metropolitan one-bank town" is used for banks in areas designated as metropolitan by the Bureau of the Census. Furthermore, these banks are in cities or suburbs with only one banking office.
Source: Table A–6 of the Statistical Appendix.

DESCRIPTION OF OPERATING RATIOS USED TO MEASURE

COMPARATIVE OPERATING CHARACTERISTICS

The measures of bank operating performance used in this analysis are the following 11 operating ratios prepared by the Board of Governors of the Federal Reserve System: [1]

A. Profitability
1. $\dfrac{\text{Net current earnings}}{\text{Total assets}}$
2. $\dfrac{\text{Net current earnings}}{\text{Total capital accounts}}$
B. Sources of revenue
1. $\dfrac{\text{Interest and dividends on government securities}}{\text{Total operating revenue}}$

1. "Member Bank Operating Ratios, Year 1964," FR 456 (Rev. 11–64), Board of Governors of the Federal Reserve System.

$$\begin{array}{l} \text{2. } \dfrac{\text{Interest and dividends on other securities}}{\text{Total operating revenue}} \\[1em] \text{3. } \dfrac{\text{Revenue on loans}}{\text{Total operating revenue}} \\[1em] \text{4. } \dfrac{\text{Service charges on deposit accounts}}{\text{Total operating revenue}} \\[1em] \text{5. } \dfrac{\text{All other revenue}}{\text{Total operating revenue}} \end{array}$$

C. Asset structure

$$\begin{array}{l} \text{1. } \dfrac{\text{Government securities}}{\text{Total assets}} \\[1em] \text{2. } \dfrac{\text{Other securities}}{\text{Total assets}} \\[1em] \text{3. } \dfrac{\text{Loans (net)}}{\text{Total assets}} \\[1em] \text{4. } \dfrac{\text{Cash assets}}{\text{Total assets}} \end{array}$$

Although these ratios are largely self-explanatory, several observations should be made.

1. The profit ratios use the figure for "Net current earnings" submitted by each bank in its "Report of Income and Dividends." This figure is a realistic measure of current operating performance because it is not affected by reported gains or losses incurred in the disposal of assets, reserve adjustments, or differential taxes.

2. It may be argued that profit ratios of small banks are unrealistic because certain salary payments and other expenses that benefit the owners should be considered part of bank profits. Such an argument may be valid in comparing the reporting practices of small and large banks. However, this analysis compares similar groups of small banks, and there is no reason to assume that, on average, reported earnings of nonpar banks are understated in comparison with those of similar par banks.

3. Included in the category "All other revenue" is income from various commissions and fees. Also included in this category are *exchange charges.*

4. The five ratios outlining sources of revenue account for 100 per cent of total operating revenue.

5. The asset figures used in these operating ratios are averages

based on three Reports of Condition (December 20, 1963; April 15, 1964; and June 30, 1964).

6. The category "Other securities" consists largely of obligations of states and political subdivisions.[2]

7. The category "Cash assets" consists principally of balances with other banks.[3]

8. The four asset ratios account for almost 100 per cent of total assets. The small discrepancy is due to the fact that bank premises are carried as an asset.

Throughout the subsequent comparative analysis of operating ratios, the figures used are averages. Technically these figures are the means of the reported ratios in each group, which are expressed as percentages. For example, on the average, the 50 nonpar banks in rural one-bank towns in Alabama had net current earnings amounting to 1.7 per cent of total assets in 1964.

While the 50 nonpar banks in rural one-bank towns in Alabama had net current earnings of 1.7 per cent of total assets, the group of 18 similar par banks had net current earnings of 1.4 per cent of total assets. When these two groups of banks are compared, the nonpar banks are found to be, on the average, more profitable. However, one must ask whether such a difference is statistically significant. To answer this question, a two-sample T-test is used.[4] The selected level of significance is 5 per cent.

COMPARISON OF OPERATING PERFORMANCE

WITHIN EACH OF THE EIGHT STATES

Table 9 presents the mean operating ratios for similar nonpar and par banks in eight nonpar states. Where there are statistically significant differences between similar banks in the same state, the figures are in italics.

2. "Assets, Liabilities, and Capital Accounts: Commercial and Mutual Savings Banks," June 30, 1965, Report of Call No. 72, Federal Deposit Insurance Corporation, Washington, p. 2.
3. *Ibid.*
4. This is a powerful statistical test for comparing the means of two samples. However at times a significant value of T may reflect differences in the standard deviations of the two samples. See G. Udny Yule and M. G. Kendall, *An Introduction to the Theory of Statistics* (London, 1958), p. 492.

Table 9. Mean operating ratios of similar nonpar and par nonmember banks in eight nonpar states (1964)

Operating Ratio	Alabama		Arkansas	
	Par	Non-par	Par	Non-par
Net current earnings				
Total assets	1.4	1.7	1.4	1.6
Net current earnings				
Total capital accounts	14.9	15.9	14.6	14.4
Interest and dividends on government securities				
Total operating revenue	22.3	24.4	19.3	20.5
Interest and dividends on other securities				
Total operating revenue	7.3	7.1	8.4	7.6
Revenue on loans				
Total operating revenue	62.2	57.8	65.0	58.4
Service charges on deposit accounts				
Total operating revenue	**4.8**	**2.7**	3.7	3.5
All other revenue				
Total operating revenue	**3.4**	**8.1**	**3.5**	**10.1**
Government securities				
Total assets	28.6	30.5	23.0	23.4
Other securities				
Total assets	13.0	12.7	11.9	11.8
Loans (net)				
Total assets	42.7	39.3	42.9	43.6
Cash assets				
Total assets	**14.4**	**16.6**	20.9	20.5
Total number of banks	18	50	21	73

Note: Figures in boldface are those that are significantly different, based on the two-sample T-test.

Source: Special tabulation prepared by the Federal Deposit Insurance Corporation, 1966.

In none of the eight states is there any significant difference in the profitability of nonpar and par banks, when measured by the ratio of *Net current earnings/Total assets.* However, when profitability is measured by *Net current earnings/Total capital accounts,* significant differences appear in four of the eight states. In North Carolina, Tennessee, and Texas the nonpar banks are significantly *less* profitable than similar par banks. In South Carolina the nonpar banks are *more* profitable than similar par banks—a finding probably related to the

Table 9. *Continued*

Florida		Missouri		North Carolina		South Carolina		Tennessee		Texas	
Par	Non-par	Par	Non-par	Par	Non-par	Par	Non-par	Par	Non-par	Par	Non-par
1.3	1.4	1.5	1.4	1.6	1.4	1.4	1.7	1.4	1.3	1.5	1.4
16.1	15.0	14.5	14.2	17.5	14.1	11.8	13.6	15.6	13.1	14.6	12.1
24.3	32.4	29.6	23.8	16.5	19.1	20.9	18.3	20.0	20.5	16.9	23.3
5.6	4.6	4.5	3.4	10.3	9.5	9.2	8.8	8.1	6.5	6.5	6.0
56.4	44.9	60.9	63.0	62.8	57.2	57.0	53.1	68.3	66.0	68.5	60.0
9.1	6.8	2.8	1.8	5.8	3.7	9.6	4.7	2.1	1.4	5.6	4.3
4.7	11.3	2.2	7.9	4.2	10.5	3.2	15.1	1.5	5.6	2.5	6.4
35.1	44.1	35.0	31.3	20.9	22.1	27.8	23.2	24.3	22.3	21.0	28.4
9.2	7.3	7.0	5.4	18.1	16.4	17.4	17.5	12.1	10.4	10.3	8.7
40.8	29.6	43.1	47.6	43.3	42.5	39.4	41.4	47.3	49.3	47.4	40.3
12.8	17.7	14.3	14.5	15.5	17.3	14.1	16.7	15.2	17.1	20.0	21.5
28	27	208	42	12	38	10	34	64	47	170	24

fact that nonpar banks in that state seem to place the greatest emphasis on exchange charges as a source of revenue (Table 13).

Examining the sources of revenue, one finds that in each of the eight states the ratio of *All other revenue/Total operating revenue* is significantly greater for the nonpar banks. This is as one might expect, because the category "All other revenue" includes income from exchange charges.

For nonpar banks in Alabama, Florida, Missouri, and South Carolina, service charges on deposit accounts are a significantly less important source of revenue than they are for similar par banks. In the other four states there is no significant difference between similar nonpar and par banks when measured by the ratio of *Service charges on deposit accounts/Total operating revenue.*

Although similar nonpar and par banks are found to differ concerning exchange charges ("All other revenue") and service charges on deposit accounts, one finds significantly different patterns in only two of the eight nonpar states when examining revenue from securities and revenue from loans. The nonpar banks in Florida and Texas receive a significantly *greater* percentage of total operating revenue from interest and dividends on government securities and a significantly *smaller* percentage of total operating revenue from income on loans. These revenue relationships for nonpar banks in Florida and Texas are clearly confirmed by the asset ratios, the banks having significantly more of their total assets in government securities and less of their total assets in loans.

In contrast to this finding for Florida and Texas, the data suggest, although less strongly, the opposite situation in Missouri. In that state a significantly smaller proportion of the total operating revenue of the nonpar banks comes from interest and dividends on government securities. Their revenue from loans is greater, but not significantly greater, than is the case for the par banks. Confirming these revenue relationships, the asset ratios show that loans constitute a significantly greater percentage of total assets for the nonpar banks in Missouri.

The ratio of *Cash assets/Total assets* provides the only other statistically significant differences in Table 9. In Alabama and Florida the nonpar banks have a significantly greater percentage of their total assets in cash items, the principal component of which is correspondent balances. While this ratio is significantly different in only two of the eight states, it is seen that in seven of the eight states the nonpar banks hold a greater percentage of their total assets in cash items. This consistent relationship implies that there may be pressures on nonpar banks leading them to maintain larger correspondent balances than do similar par banks. This question of correspondent balances is examined in Chapter IX.

Some critics of nonpar banking allege that a nonpar bank, because it has a steady stream of income from exchange charges, is likely to hold many government securities and to be less progressive in meeting the legitimate borrowing needs of its community.[5] Based on the preceding analysis, such an allegation must be generally rejected. In only two of the eight states (Florida and Texas) does the comparative analysis

5. Clifton H. Kreps, Jr., "Characteristics of Nonpar Banks: A Case Study," *The Southern Economic Journal*, XXVI (July 1959), 49.

Table 10. Nonmember banks in nonpar states reporting *no* revenue from service charges on deposit accounts, classified by structure of local competition (1964)

Structure of Local Competition	Nonpar		Par	
	Number of Banks	Per-centage *	Number of Banks	Per-centage *
Rural one-bank town				
Alabama	11	22	4	19
Arkansas	12	16	3	12
Florida	0	——	0	——
Missouri	13	30	34	16
North Carolina	6	16	1	8
South Carolina	3	9	0	——
Tennessee	17	36	19	30
Texas	2	8	14	8
Total (eight states)	64	19	75	14
Georgia	13	12	——	——
Louisiana	1	2	——	——
Minnesota	27	9	——	——
Mississippi	6	9	——	——
North Dakota	9	11	——	——
South Dakota	6	7	——	——
Total (six states)	62	9	——	——
Competing nonpar facility in town	28	12	——	——
Competing par facility in town	7	10	——	——
Metropolitan one-bank town	9	11	——	——
Total nonpar banks	170	12	——	——

* These percentage calculations relate to the total in each category shown in Table A–6, Statistical Appendix.

Source: Special tabulation prepared by the Federal Deposit Insurance Corporation, 1966.

tend to confirm this alleged pattern of behavior. The findings for Missouri suggest the opposite situation, and in the other five states no significant differences are found in the lending and investing policies of similar nonpar and par banks.

The principal distinction between these two groups of banks is that nonpar banks, having income from exchange charges, in general rely less on service charges on deposit accounts as a source of revenue.

Table 11. Mean operating ratios of nonpar banks in rural one-bank towns in six states (1964)

Operating Ratio	Georgia	Louisiana	Minnesota	Mississippi	North Dakota	South Dakota
Net current earnings						
Total assets	1.6	1.3	1.0	1.3	1.4	1.5
Net current earnings						
Total capital accounts	15.1	16.1	11.0	15.4	14.8	14.6
Interest and dividends on government securities						
Total operating revenue	25.5	23.6	24.5	15.6	28.8	26.3
Interest and dividends on other securities						
Total operating revenue	4.5	10.5	5.7	12.0	8.7	4.6
Revenue on loans						
Total operating revenue	55.6	51.5	55.8	58.1	47.7	56.0
Service charges on deposit accounts						
Total operating revenue	3.8	4.9	3.5	4.4	2.7	3.4
All other revenue						
Total operating revenue	10.5	9.5	10.5	10.0	12.1	9.6
Government securities						
Total assets	31.7	30.4	32.4	19.4	34.2	34.8
Other securities						
Total assets	10.3	14.7	10.0	16.6	13.8	7.6
Loans (net)						
Total assets	39.5	33.6	45.8	43.4	41.4	46.0
Cash assets						
Total assets	17.7	20.4	11.0	19.2	9.8	10.8
Total number of banks	112	49	306	70	84	91

Source: Special tabulation prepared by the Federal Deposit Insurance Corporation, 1966.

Another major distinction is that nonpar banks have a consistently greater percentage of their total assets in cash, the principal component of which is correspondent balances.

Although usually a smaller percentage of the total operating revenue of nonpar banks comes from service charges on deposit accounts, most nonpar banks do report some revenue from this source. Table 10 indicates the number and percentage of nonpar banks reporting no revenue from service charges on deposit accounts. In the eight selected nonpar states 19 per cent of the nonpar banks report no revenue from service charges on deposit accounts. This figure is not very different from that of similar par banks in the same eight states, 14 per cent of which report no revenue from such service charges.

EVALUATION OF OPERATING RATIOS FOR NONPAR BANKS

IN RURAL ONE-BANK TOWNS IN SIX STATES

As shown in Table 6, there are six states in which the number of similar par banks is too small to be used for comparative purposes. Table 11 presents the mean operating ratios for selected nonpar banks in these six states. While the nonpar banks cannot be compared directly with similar par banks in the same states, several observations should be made about them.

The profitability of the nonpar banks in Minnesota is noticeably lower than that of similar nonpar banks in the other states. This is evident in each of the two ratios measuring profitability. That this finding is a state phenomenon is confirmed by the fact that in North Dakota and South Dakota the profitability of similar nonpar banks is higher, more like the profitability of similar nonpar banks in the southern states. The reason for the lower level of profits in the Minnesota nonpar banks has not been identified in this study.

In each of the three nonpar states in the upper Middle West the nonpar banks have noticeably lower ratios of *Cash assets/Total assets* than do similar nonpar banks in the southern states. As noted, "Cash assets" in this ratio consist principally of correspondent balances. These regional variations in correspondent balances may be explained by related regional differences in policies concerning absorption of exchange charges (Chapter IX).

41

Table 12. Mean operating ratios of nonpar and par banks in fourteen nonpar states, classified by structure of local competition (1964)

Operating Ratio	Nonmember Par Banks in Eight States *	Nonpar Banks in Eight States *	Nonpar Banks in Six States *	Competing Nonpar Facility in Town	Competing Par Facility in Town	Metropolitan One-Bank Town
Net current earnings						
Total assets	1.5	1.5	1.2	1.3	1.3	1.3
Net current earnings						
Total capital accounts	14.8	14.2	13.3	15.1	15.0	14.0
Interest and dividends on government securities						
Total operating revenue	23.0	22.3	24.4	21.2	23.0	22.5
Interest and dividends on other securities						
Total operating revenue	6.1	6.8	6.7	7.6	8.1	6.4
Revenue on loans						
Total operating revenue	64.2	58.3	54.8	58.0	55.8	53.9
Service charges on deposit accounts						
Total operating revenue	4.2	3.3	3.7	4.2	5.0	5.1
All other revenue						
Total operating revenue	2.5	9.3	10.4	8.9	8.0	12.0
Government securities						
Total assets	28.1	27.1	31.4	27.2	28.1	29.5
Other securities						
Total assets	9.6	11.5	11.2	12.7	13.8	12.0
Loans (net)						
Total assets	44.8	42.5	43.2	43.2	41.1	42.8
Cash assets						
Total assets	16.4	17.8	13.4	15.6	15.8	14.4
Total number of banks	531	335	712	237	68	79

* The banks in these categories are located in rural one-bank towns.

Note: Figures in boldface are those that are significantly different, based on the two-sample T-test, from the control group of 335 nonpar banks in rural one-bank towns in eight states.

COMPARISON OF OPERATING CHARACTERISTICS OF

AGGREGATE NONPAR BANKS, CLASSIFIED BY

VARIOUS STRUCTURES OF COMPETITION

The preceding ratio analysis compares similar nonpar and par banks within the same state. In addition, several observations are made concerning nonpar banks in states where there is not a sufficient number of similar par banks for comparative purposes. The preceding examination of certain operating characteristics of nonpar banks in rural one-bank towns accounts for 71 per cent of all nonpar banks.

In Table 12 the selected operating ratios are presented on an aggregate basis, these aggregates being classified by structure of local competition. The two-sample T-test has been used in this table, again at the 5 per cent level of significance. The control group for the aggregate comparisons consists of the nonpar banks in the eight selected states. Because these aggregates are necessarily based on the merging of data for nonpar banks in various states, findings of statistically significant differences between aggregates must be viewed with more caution than the preceding findings based on comparisons within states.

Concerning the nonpar banks in rural one-bank towns, these aggregate comparisons basically confirm the previous findings within states.

In the eight selected states there is no significant difference in the aggregate profitability of nonpar and par banks in rural one-bank towns. While this is true in the aggregate, certain significant differences in profitability within these states have been previously noted.

Concerning sources of revenue, the aggregate comparisons for the eight states confirm the earlier findings that nonpar banks place significantly greater reliance on exchange income than do par banks and significantly less reliance on service charges on deposit accounts.

In the aggregate one finds that the nonpar banks in the eight states place less reliance on loans than do similar par banks. This finding is based on the two loan ratios: *Revenue on loans/Total operating revenue* and *Loans (net)/Total assets*. Because these aggregate loan ratios are based on data merged for several states, the findings must be regarded as tentative. When the loan ratios are compared within states, only in Texas and Florida are the nonpar banks found to place significantly less reliance on loans (Table 9).

In the aggregate the nonpar banks in the eight states have a significantly greater percentage of their total assets in the form of "Cash assets" (correspondent balances). This relationship has been noted in the comparisons within states. Also, in the comparison of aggregates the nonpar banks in the eight states have a significantly greater percentage of total assets in the form of "Other securities." Such a finding does not appear in any of the comparisons within states, and its appearance in the aggregate comparisons is a statistical anomaly.[6]

When the nonpar banks in the eight states are used as a control group, the selected operating ratios of these 335 banks may be compared with the ratios of the 712 similar nonpar banks in the other six states.

The nonpar banks in the six states are significantly less profitable than are the nonpar banks in the eight states. This is largely explained by the fact that the nonpar banks in Minnesota account for 43 per cent of the nonpar banks in the six states; and, as previously observed, the average profitability of these nonpar banks in Minnesota is noticeably lower than that of similar nonpar banks in other states.

For the 712 nonpar banks in the six states, the category "All other revenue" accounts for a significantly greater percentage of their total operating revenue. This finding, developed in the next chapter, is largely explained by the fact that nonpar banks in the upper Middle West receive revenue from insurance affiliates and other miscellaneous sources, and such revenue is reported in this category.

In contrast to the 335 nonpar banks in the eight states, the 712 nonpar banks in the six states have a significantly greater percentage of their total assets in government securities, and the interest and dividends from such securities provide a significantly greater percentage of the total operating revenue of the 712 banks. While the revenue from government securities is significantly greater for the 712 banks, their revenue from loans is significantly less. However, there is no significant difference between the group of 335 banks and the group of 712 banks when measured by the ratio of *Loans (net)/Total assets*. Where there is a significant difference between these two groups of banks, it is found in the proportion of cash items to total assets. This finding in the aggregate comparison confirms the earlier observation that nonpar banks in the upper Middle West maintain a noticeably lower percentage of total assets in the form of correspondent balances than do nonpar banks in the southern states.

6. The explanation is that in the states where this ratio is low the par banks predominate; in states where this ratio is high the nonpar banks predominate. Merging the data results in the significant difference in the aggregate.

As measured by the ratio of *Net current earnings/Total assets,* nonpar banks facing local competition and nonpar banks in metropolitan one-bank towns are significantly less profitable than the 335 nonpar banks in rural one-bank towns.[7] However, as measured by the ratio of *Net current earnings/Total capital accounts,* nonpar banks facing local competition are more profitable than the control group of banks. The apparent inconsistency of these measures may indicate that, on the average, nonpar banks facing local competition have lower ratios of capital to total assets.

Nonpar banks facing local competition and nonpar banks in metropolitan one-bank towns derive a significantly greater percentage of their total operating revenue from service charges on deposit accounts than do the banks in the control group. As shown in Table 10, 88 per cent of all nonpar banks report some revenue from service charges on deposit accounts. However, given their stream of revenue from exchange charges, some nonpar banks may purposely establish lower service charges than their local par competitors and advertise these lower service charges in order to attract additional accounts.

Compared with the 335 banks in the control group, nonpar banks facing par competition obtain a significantly *smaller* percentage of their total operating revenue from the category "All other revenue." This finding relates well to the analysis in Chapter VII, which demonstrates how a local par bank may sometimes benefit at the expense of its nonpar competitor. In comparison with the control group, the nonpar banks in metropolitan one-bank towns obtain a significantly *greater* percentage of their total operating revenue from the category "All other revenue." This finding is further developed in Chapter IX.

Compared with the control group, nonpar banks facing local competition and nonpar banks in metropolitan one-bank towns are not significantly different in the percentage of their total operating revenue from these sources: (1) interest and dividends from government securities, (2) interest and dividends from other securities, and (3) revenue on loans (except for the nonpar banks in metropolitan one-bank towns). Similarly, the asset ratios indicate no significant differences between these groups of banks in their proportions of total assets in (1) government securities, (2) other securities, and (3) loans (net). The only significant differences in the asset ratios between these groups of nonpar banks and the control group is the percentage

7. The classification "metropolitan one-bank town" is used for banks in areas designated as metropolitan by the Bureau of the Census. Furthermore, these banks are in cities or suburbs with only one banking office.

of total assets held in cash items. Nonpar banks facing local competition and located in metropolitan one-bank towns hold a smaller percentage of their total assets as correspondent balances than do the 335 nonpar banks in rural one-bank towns. Yet these correspondent balances may be larger than those of similar par banks facing local competition or located in metropolitan one-bank towns. However, such a comparison is not made in this study.

CONCLUSIONS

In nonpar states similar par banks exist and are as profitable as nonpar banks. (By one measure of profitability the par banks in some states are more profitable than are similar nonpar banks.) This finding is not in itself a sufficient reason for nonpar banks to become par banks, but it is of considerable importance if one finds that nonpar banking imposes a major cost burden on other banks, corporations, and individuals in the economy. Chapter X analyzes and measures this cost burden.

Nonpar banks place greater reliance on exchange charges and less reliance on service charges on deposit accounts as a source of revenue. (The contribution of exchange charges to the total current operating revenue of nonpar banks is analyzed in Chapter VI.) Although 88 per cent of the nonpar banks report some revenue from service charges on deposit accounts, nonpar banks, on the average, do not act as profit maximizers by charging exchange and also having a level of service charges comparable with that of similar par banks.

Nonpar banks generally have a greater percentage of total assets in the form of correspondent balances. (Probable reasons for this finding are discussed in Chapters VII and IX.) By becoming par institutions, many nonpar banks may be able to convert such excess nonearning correspondent balances into earning assets—as did those banks that changed from nonpar to par in 1962–63 (Chapter VIII).

In general, nonpar banks are not found to differ from similar par banks in their lending and investing policies. As measured by the ratios of *Loans (net)/Total assets* and *Revenue on loans/Total operating revenue,* the average nonpar bank seems to be adequately serving the borrowing needs of its community.

VI

The Importance
of Exchange Income
to Nonpar Banks

The principal question considered in this chapter is how much do exchange charges currently contribute to the total operating revenue of nonpar banks.[1] Also, the current contribution of exchange charges is compared with their past importance as a source of revenue for nonpar banks. The information developed in this analysis provides a factual basis for evaluating what the probable impact on nonpar banks would be if the practice of charging exchange were discontinued.

Lack of data has impeded attempts to analyze the magnitude of exchange charges in the nation's banking system. One reason for this lack of data is that income from exchange charges is consolidated with other sources of revenue in the "Report of Income and Dividends," prepared annually by each insured bank and submitted to the bank supervisory authority. This composite figure is reported in item 1(e): "Other service charges, commissions, fees, and collection and exchange charges."[2] Thus when considering the figure reported by nonpar banks in item 1(e), one must recognize that this reported figure may exceed the amount of income from exchange charges because such income is only one component of the composite figure. Despite this limitation, analysis of the data reported by banks in item 1(e) is useful because it provides a measure of the maximum possible income from exchange charges.

1. The banks analyzed in this chapter are all nonpar banks insured by the Federal Deposit Insurance Corporation.
2. "Report of Income and Dividends—Calendar Year 1964," Form 73, Federal Deposit Insurance Corporation.

47

CURRENT MAXIMUM CONTRIBUTION OF EXCHANGE

INCOME TO TOTAL OPERATING REVENUE OF VARIOUS

NONPAR BANKS

Table 13 provides a distribution of item 1(e), "Other service charges, commissions, fees, and collection and exchange charges," as a per-

Table 13. Revenue from "other service charges, commissions, fees, and collection and exchange charges" as a percentage of "total current operating revenue" of nonpar banks, classified by state and by deposit size (1964)

	Deposit Size (millions of dollars)					
State	Under 1	1–2	2–5	5–10	10–25 *	All Banks
Alabama	7.3	6.4	6.9	5.1	7.6	6.5
Arkansas	11.7	9.6	8.1	8.9	3.2	9.0
Florida	14.5	7.7	9.7	9.2	——	9.6
Georgia	10.2	9.6	9.3	7.9	6.7	9.3
Louisiana	11.5	7.8	6.5	7.2	6.4	7.4
Minnesota	13.7	10.6	9.7	8.8	11.5	10.3
Mississippi	11.2	8.3	8.0	7.4	7.6	8.0
Missouri	7.4	6.0	8.1	6.2	——	7.2
North Carolina	——	10.6	8.3	10.8	10.3	9.3
North Dakota	14.9	12.5	10.9	11.7	——	11.7
South Carolina	17.3	15.0	13.3	——	8.3	14.0
South Dakota	12.8	8.8	8.1	8.6	——	8.9
Tennessee	4.9	4.9	4.9	3.7	3.2	4.7
Texas	5.6	7.3	5.1	——	——	6.1
All banks	11.1	9.6	8.8	7.8	7.0	9.1

* Only 25 banks are in this deposit-size category.

Source: Special tabulation prepared by the Federal Deposit Insurance Corporation, 1966.

centage of the "Total current operating revenue" of nonpar banks. This distribution by state and by deposit size presents the mean ratio for the banks in each cell.

A number of findings emerge from this tabulation:

There is greater variation by state than by deposit-size classification. The mean percentage for all nonpar banks is 9.1. By state the mean percentage ranges from 4.7 to 14.0; by deposit size, from 7.0 to 11.1.

For banks with under $1,000,000 in deposits the percentage is consistently, and usually considerably, larger than it is for banks in the larger deposit-size categories. Of the 14 states only Tennessee and Texas are exceptions to this finding.

In the aggregate, the percentage contribution of item 1(e) to total current operating revenue declines as the size of the bank increases. There are, however, exceptions within states. For example, in Arkansas, Louisiana, North Carolina, North Dakota, and South Dakota the percentage figure is larger for banks with from $5,000,000 to $10,-000,000 in deposits than it is for banks with from $2,000,000 to $5,000,000.

Because the preceding analysis has been based on averages, some measures of dispersion are useful to clarify further the importance of item 1(e) to the total current operating revenue of nonpar banks. Table A–7 in the Statistical Appendix shows by state that 66 per cent of the nonpar banks report less than 10 per cent of their total current operating revenue in item 1(e). Only 3 per cent of the nonpar banks report more than 20 per cent of their total current operating revenue in item 1(e).

CHANGES IN THE MAXIMUM CONTRIBUTION OF EXCHANGE INCOME TO TOTAL OPERATING REVENUE OF NONPAR BANKS: 1942–64

Although item 1(e) as a percentage of total current operating revenue varies more by state than by deposit size, such data by state are not available for earlier years. A study made by the Federal Deposit Insurance Corporation in 1942 includes a distribution by deposit size.[3] This distribution has been used in Table 14, which compares the data by deposit size for 1942 and 1964, and shows how the role of exchange charges has changed through time.

In 1942 the revenue reported in item 1(e) accounted for 19 per cent of the total current operating revenue of all insured nonpar banks in 27 states. In 1964 the figure was 9 per cent for all insured nonpar banks in 14 states. Thus over this 22-year period the percentage

3. The year 1942 in a sense may not be typical. However, it is the only year of that period for which such a distribution is available. Therefore the distribution is compared to that of 1964 to learn whether there have been broad changes through time.

Table 14. Revenue from "other service charges, commissions, fees, and collection and exchange charges" as a percentage of "total current operating revenue" of nonpar banks, classified by deposit size and by the years 1942 and 1964

Deposit Size (millions of dollars)	1942 (27 States)		1964 (14 States)	
	Per-centage	Number of Banks	Per-centage	Number of Banks
Under 1.0 *	——	——	11.1	139
0.5–1.0 (1942 data)	19.0	698	——	——
1.0–2.0	18.0	267	9.6	460
2.0–5.0	19.0	76	8.8	657
5.0–10.0	25.0	9	7.8	191
10.0–25.0 *	——	——	7.0	25
10.0–50.0 (1942 data)	15.0	4	——	——
Total	19.0†	2,415†	9.1	1,472‡

* Where deposit-size categories in the study of 1942 differ from those used in this study, they are noted, and the most comparable category has been selected for comparative purposes.

† Includes 1,361 banks with deposits of less than $500,000 in 1942. These banks are not included in the above distribution.

‡ Excludes one bank having over $25,000,000 in deposits.

Source: Table 13 and *Hearings, Absorption of Exchange Charges*, p. 723.

contribution of item 1(e) to the total current operating revenue of all nonpar banks decreased by more than 50 per cent.

The decrease has been greater for larger nonpar banks than for smaller nonpar banks. For nonpar banks with deposits from $5,000,000 to $10,000,000 the percentage contribution fell from 25.0 to 7.8—a 69 per cent decrease. For nonpar banks with deposits of $500,000 to $1,000,000 the percentage contribution fell from 19.0 to 11.1—a 42 per cent decrease.

These findings clearly demonstrate that the percentage contribution of item 1(e) to the total current operating revenue of nonpar banks has declined greatly over the past two decades.

MAXIMUM EXCHANGE INCOME OF ALL NONPAR BANKS

Having determined the contribution of item 1(e) to the total current operating revenue of various nonpar banks, it is necessary to consider the *aggregate* amount reported in item 1(e) by *all* nonpar banks. Table 15 presents the total amount of revenue reported in item

Table 15. Total income reported in item 1(e),
"other service charges, commissions, fees, and
collection and exchange charges," by all nonpar
banks, classified by state (1964)

State	Total Income Reported in Item 1(e) (thousands of dollars)
Alabama	818
Arkansas	1,000
Florida	632
Georgia	3,265
Louisiana	1,738
Minnesota	5,665
Mississippi	2,131
Missouri	455
North Carolina	979
North Dakota	1,673
South Carolina	746
South Dakota	1,107
Tennessee	382
Texas	101
Total	20,692

Source: Special tabulation prepared by the
Federal Deposit Insurance Corporation, 1966.

1(e) by all nonpar banks in each of the nonpar states. The revenue reported under item 1(e) by all insured nonpar banks in the nation was $20,700,000 in 1964. The largest amount was reported in Minnesota, and three states—Georgia, Minnesota, and Mississippi—account for over 50 per cent of the national total. Again one must recognize that this figure of $20,700,000 exceeds the actual amount of exchange income to the nonpar banks. However, it does provide a useful maximum.

ESTIMATED EXCHANGE INCOME OF ALL NONPAR BANKS

Having worked with the composite item 1(e) as a maximum, it is desirable to estimate the actual role of exchange charges in this composite figure.

In its 1942 study the Federal Deposit Insurance Corporation looked at the income reported is item 1(e) by nonpar banks and by nonmember par banks in the nonpar states.[4] This income from item 1(e) was standardized by deposit size and measured against the total earnings and total assets of the banks involved. The Federal Deposit Insurance Corporation "assumed that the differences between the rates for these [par] banks and for the nonpar banks were due to the exchange charged by the latter for remitting funds to distant points."[5] For convenience, the study by the Federal Deposit Insurance Corporation thereafter referred to this difference—the excess which the nonpar banks received [as reported in item 1(e)] over that which the par banks received—as "remittance exchange."[6]

Given the data available at the time, the analytical procedure used by the Federal Deposit Insurance Corporation was a worthwhile attempt to estimate the role of exchange charges in the composite item 1(e). However, one may question the assumption that the difference between the rates reported by nonpar banks and nonmember par banks is due basically to exchange charges. At the logical extreme, given their revenue from exchange charges, nonpar banks may seldom inaugurate other customer charges reported in item 1(e). On this assumption, all revenue reported in item 1(e) by nonpar banks is from exchange charges. Nonmember par banks, not having such exchange revenue, may adopt other customer charges, reported as revenue in item 1(e). On the basis of these assumptions, the total figure reported in item 1(e) by nonpar banks may be a better estimate of the role of exchange charges for nonpar banks.

Because of uncertainties as to the role of exchange charges in item 1(e) as reported by nonpar banks, in 1966 the Federal Deposit Insurance Corporation conducted a special survey in 10 of the 14 nonpar states to obtain more precise information about income from exchange charges. These 10 states are listed in Table A–8 of the Statistical Appendix, together with information concerning the number of banks surveyed in each state. The nonpar banks in the 10 states reported $17,200,000 of revenue in item 1(e) in 1964, thus accounting for 83 per cent of the total revenue of $20,700,000 reported in item 1(e) by all nonpar banks in 1964 (Table 15).

A brief survey was completed by the examiners of the Federal Deposit Insurance Corporation during their regular examination of each nonmember bank in the 10 selected nonpar states. This survey,

---

4. Some aspects of this study are discussed in Chapter III.
5. U. S. Congress, House Committee on Banking and Currency, *Hearings on H.R.3956, Absorption of Exchange Charges,* 78th Cong., 2d Sess., 1943–44, p. 716.
6. *Ibid.*

conducted during the three-month period from April 1 through June 30, 1966, provides an approximate 25 per cent sample of nonmember banks in the 10 states. This sample may be assumed to be random for three reasons: (1) The nature of bank examination requires that scheduled examinations be basically random to avoid patterns that might be observed by the banks to be examined. (2) The examinations during the three-month period were prescheduled and therefore not selected on the basis of this survey. (3) Certain empirical checks were made with the Examination Division to confirm the basic randomness of the examination schedule.

An objective of this survey was to separate the various components of item 1(e). Of principal importance was identification of the amount of exchange charges against checks presented by mail for payment. In addition, it was desired to identify the other major sources of revenue that comprise the total figure reported in item 1(e) of the "Report of Income and Dividends." Exhibit A–1 in the Appendix is a copy of the form used in this special "Survey of Par Clearance."

The information yielded by the survey enabled the Federal Deposit Insurance Corporation to calculate the income from exchange charges as a percentage of the total revenue reported in item 1(e) in 1965. These percentage relationships were classified in four categories, as shown in Table 16. Here one learns that for 54 per cent of the banks in this survey, exchange charges accounted for 75–100 per cent of the total revenue reported in item 1(e) in 1965. Moreover, considering only the 165 banks in the seven southern states, one observes that for 76 per cent of these banks, exchange charges accounted for 75–100 per cent of the total revenue reported in item 1(e) in 1965. These findings indicate that for most nonpar banks in six of the selected nonpar states, the figure reported for item 1(e) closely reflects the actual revenue from exchange charges.

By examining the distributions in Table 16, one is able to select the category that includes the median for each state. The midpoint of each such selected category is used as an estimate of the typical relationship of exchange income as a percentage of the revenue reported in item 1(e). When the midpoint has been selected, this figure is rounded down to the nearest figure expressible as a multiple of 5 per cent. For example, 85.0 per cent is used as an estimate for Alabama, rather than the midpoint of 87.5 per cent.

Using the above procedure, one finds that in six of the seven southern states 85 per cent of the figure reported in item 1(e) is typically revenue from exchange charges. The seventh state, Florida, has few nonpar banks, so the estimate of 60 per cent for this state is necessarily an approximation based on the sample of seven banks.

For the nonpar banks in Minnesota, North Dakota, and South Dakota, the figure reported in item 1(e) often includes important

Table 16. Exchange charges as a percentage of item 1(e), "other service charges' commissions, fees, and collection and exchange charges," of nonpar banks, classified by the nonpar states included in the "Survey of Par Clearance" (1965)

Selected Nonpar States	Exchange Charges as a Percentage of Revenue Reported in Item 1(e)				Total Number of Banks Surveyed	Estimate of "Typical" Percentage Relationship *
	Under 25	25–50	50–75	75–100		
Alabama	——	1	——	12	13	85
Arkansas	1	1	2	16	20	85
Florida	——	1	3	3	7	60
Georgia	——	5	5	55	65	85
Minnesota	4	33	35	32	104	60
Mississippi	1	6	3	23	33	85
Missouri	1	——	1	5	7	85
North Dakota	1	6	13	6	26	60
South Dakota	——	5	8	5	18	60
Tennessee	2	4	2	12	20	85
Total	10	62	72	169	313	——

* This "typical" percentage relationship is estimated by surveying the distribution of each state, selecting the midpoint of the appropriate category, and rounding down to the nearest figure expressible as a multiple of 5 per cent.

Source: The distribution by categories is from a special tabulation prepared by the Federal Deposit Insurance Corporation, 1966.

sources of revenue in addition to exchange charges. Many nonpar banks in these three states operate insurance agencies in conjunction with their banking operations, and the income from such insurance affiliates is often a major component of the revenue reported in item 1(e). Other typical sources of revenue reported in item 1(e) are the following: [7]

A. Charges to depositors for overdrafts and returned checks.
B. Charges for nonpar checks drawn on other banks and presented for cash or deposit.
C. Rent from lease of bank property and safe-deposit boxes.

7. Special tabulation prepared by the Federal Deposit Insurance Corporation, Washington, 1966.

D. Various fees [for]
   1. Collecting utility bills.
   2. Issuing money orders.
   3. Notarizing documents.
   4. Preparing income tax forms.
   5. Servicing real estate.
   6. Serving auctions.

These diverse sources of revenue reported in item 1(e) by nonpar banks in the three states help explain this study's estimate that 60 per cent of the figure reported in item 1(e) is typically income from exchange charges (Table 16).

The estimated percentage relationships presented in Table 16 are based on figures for 1965. Assuming that these percentage relationships are substantially the same as those existing in 1964, one can refine the earlier maximum of $20,700,000 as the total revenue from

Table 17. Estimate of total income from exchange charges received by all nonpar banks, classified by state (1964)

State	Total Income Reported in Item 1(e) (thousands of dollars)	Estimate of Typical Percentage Relationship *	Estimate of Total Income from Exchange Charges (thousands of dollars)
Alabama	818	85	695
Arkansas	1,000	85	850
Florida	632	60	379
Georgia	3,265	85	2,775
Louisiana	1,738	85 *	1,477
Minnesota	5,665	60	3,399
Mississippi	2,131	85	1,811
Missouri	455	85	387
North Carolina	979	85 *	832
North Dakota	1,673	60	1,004
South Carolina	746	85 *	634
South Dakota	1,107	60	664
Tennessee	382	85	325
Texas	101	85 *	86
Total	20,692	——	15,318

* For the four southern states not covered in the special survey, the assumption is made that 85 per cent is the typical percentage relationship, as is generally found for the other southern nonpar states.

Source: Tables 15 and 16.

exchange charges for all nonpar banks in 1964. Such a refined estimate is developed in Table 17, where it is estimated that exchange charges provided about $15,300,000 in revenue for all nonpar banks in 1964. Concerning the nonpar banks in the four states not covered in the special survey, if—in contrast to the procedure used in Table 17—one assumes that 100 per cent of the revenue reported in item 1(e) is from exchange charges, then the estimated revenue from exchange charges for all nonpar banks is about $15,900,000.

On the basis of the preceding analysis, it may be concluded that the practice of charging exchange produced revenue of $15,000,000 to $16,000,000 for the nation's nonpar banks in 1964. Although this range is an improvement on the maximum of $20,700,000, it may slightly overstate the actual amount of exchange income for the nonpar banks. Nevertheless the range is important, because figures developed in Chapter X demonstrate how nonpar banking is a cost burden on other banks in the nation.

VII
Changes in Nonpar Banks: 1960–64

At year-end 1959 there were 1,584 insured nonpar banks; at year-end 1964 there were 1,473. Thus during this five-year period, the total number of insured nonpar banks decreased by 111.[1] This chapter examines the various components of that aggregate decrease in nonpar banks and analyzes why banks change from nonpar to par.

Whether branch banking is permitted is a major factor in explaining changes from nonpar to par. Table A–9 in the Statistical Appendix shows the changes in nonpar banks by state during the period 1960–64 and relates these changes to the predominant banking structure in each state. Summarizing the data in Table A–9, one finds the relationships shown in Table 18.

Table 18. Total changes in nonpar banks and nonpar branches, classified by predominant banking structure (1960–64)

Predominant Structure of Banking	Percentage of Change	
	Banks	Branches
Unit banking	− 2	+19
Limited branching	− 7	+16
Statewide branching	−36	−32

Sources: Table A–9 of the Statistical Appendix. *Federal Reserve Bulletin*, XLVI (February 1960), 223. *Ibid.*, LI (February 1965), 325.

While insured nonpar banks decreased by 7 per cent during the years 1960–64, the decrease in unit-banking states was 2 per cent, and

1. These figures are from Table A–9 in the Statistical Appendix.

Table 19. Changes in nonpar banks, classified by factors contributing to change and by predominant banking structure (1960–64) *

Factors Contributing to Change	Unit Banking				Limited Branching		Statewide Branching		Total Banks	
	Upper Middle West		Four Other States †							
	Minus	Plus	Minus	Plus	Minus	Plus	Minus	Plus	Minus	Plus
Absorption	3	—	—	—	3	—	17	—	23	—
Conversion to national charter	2	—	2	—	1	—	1	—	6	—
Suspension	—	—	1	—	1	—	—	—	2	—
Changed from nonpar to par										
New par facility in town	2	—	3	—	8	—	15	—	28	—
Had competed with par facility in town	3	—	1	—	8	—	1	—	13	—
Had competed with nonpar facility in town	—	—	—	—	15	—	1	—	16	—
One-Bank town										
Metropolitan	2	—	7	—	6	—	5	—	20	—
Rural	1	—	22	—	19	—	13	—	55	—
Newly chartered nonpar	—	10	—	5	—	9	—	1	—	25
Changed from par to nonpar	—	9	—	—	—	2	—	—	—	11
Noninsured nonpar to insured nonpar	—	6	—	2	—	7	—	1	—	16
Total decrease	13		36		61		53		163	
Total increase		25		7		18		2		52
Net change	+12		−29		−43		−51		−111	

* Table A–9 of the Statistical Appendix identifies the states classified under each heading of predominant banking structure.
† Arkansas, Florida, Missouri, and Texas.
Source: Special tabulation prepared by the Federal Deposit Insurance Corporation, 1966.

the decrease in states permitting statewide branching was 36 per cent. The role of branching regulations is further suggested by the decrease in the number of nonpar branches. The only decrease in the number of nonpar branches was in the two states where statewide branching is prevalent. Why the presence or absence of branch banking results in such diverse changes in nonpar banking will be examined shortly.

The total decrease of 111 insured nonpar banks during the years 1960–64 represents an aggregate change that reflects diverse components. Table 19 classifies various factors affecting the number of nonpar banks and relates these factors to the predominant banking structure.

FACTORS REDUCING THE NUMBER OF NONPAR BANKS

Absorptions accounted for the elimination of 23 nonpar banks as separate banking institutions. Such absorptions occur principally in the two states permitting statewide branching; in fact, almost 80 per cent of the absorptions took place in these states.

It is in branch-banking states that an absorbed bank loses its individual corporate identity, although it generally continues as a branch of the absorbing bank. Thus when a nonpar bank is absorbed, the statistics record a decrease in the number of nonpar banks by one. However, an absorbed bank may continue as a nonpar branch of an absorbing nonmember bank, even when the absorbing bank is par at its main office. As explained in Chapter IV, a branch may be nonpar because of the absence of par competition in the same town.

During the years 1960–64 six nonpar banks converted from state to national charters. Since national banks must be members of the Federal Reserve System, these banks relinquished their privilege of charging exchange and thereby sacrificed a known source of revenue. It is assumed that other factors were considered to outweigh this loss.

Two nonpar banks were suspended between 1960 and 1964. It is assumed that such suspensions were unrelated to the fact that the banks were nonpar.

Three factors, then, contributed to the decline in nonpar banks: absorptions, conversions to national charters, and suspensions. It is now necessary to examine those banks that changed from nonpar to par while continuing to operate as individual nonmember banks. In the same period, 1960–64, 132 banks decided to change from nonpar to par, and in Table 19 these banks are classified by the structure of local competition.

Of the 132 banks changing from nonpar to par, 28 (21 per cent) did so shortly after the introduction of a new par facility in the community. These new par facilities were often branches, as indicated by the fact that 23 of them (over 80 per cent) were in states having some branch banking.

Of the 132 banks changing from nonpar to par, 13 (10 per cent) had been competing with a par facility for some time before deciding to become par banks. While only 5 per cent of the nonpar banks at year-end 1964 faced a par competitor in the same town, 10 per cent of the banks that changed from nonpar to par during 1960–64 faced such competition. This suggests that the situation of a nonpar and par bank in the same town is unstable and often transitional, principally because a town with a par bank (or branch) becomes a "par point."[2] Checks drawn on the nonpar bank are often sent to the par bank for collection, and the par bank presents these checks directly to the nonpar bank for full credit. The reason that the par bank in town is frequently willing to act as collecting agent is an excellent example of how each of two parties improves its position through bilateral trade.

Bank A is a large correspondent bank that processes many out-of-town checks drawn on the nonpar bank. According to the schedule of exchange charges, Bank A knows that if it sends the nonpar items directly to the nonpar bank that bank will deduct X dollars per day, on the average, in exchange charges. This X dollars per day is the cost to Bank A of direct sendings to the nonpar bank. Given this cost estimate, a representative of Bank A may call on the par bank in town and express Bank A's willingness to send the nonpar checks to the par bank for collection, allowing the par bank a credit for the amount that the nonpar bank would otherwise charge. In return, the par bank is requested to maintain a satisfactory compensating balance with Bank A—this balance having an estimated value for Bank A of Y dollars per day, on the average. Using this basic procedure, or a slight variation of it, Bank A reduces its actual cost from X dollars per day to $(X - Y)$ dollars per day. The recipient of the $(X - Y)$ dollars is the par bank.[3] Thus, through their bilateral agreement, both Bank A and the par

2. In his article "Characteristics of Nonpar Banks: A Case Study" Clifton H. Kreps, Jr., points out that the existence of a par bank in the same town "apparently . . . places almost irresistible pressure on the nonpar bank to become par-remitting also" (*The Southern Economic Journal*, XXVI [July 1959], 47). The subsequent analysis in this chapter explains why this is the case.

3. In this analysis Y is defined for Bank A (the city correspondent) as the estimated dollar value per day of the compensating balance of the par bank in town. The opportunity cost to the par bank need not be exactly the same amount.

bank improve their positions, at the expense of the nonpar bank. How much each of the two parties improves its position with respect to the other depends on Y, the value of the agreed compensating balance—this agreement in turn being a function of the relative strength and sophistication of the two parties.

Because Bank A has the option of arranging to send nonpar items through the par bank, its representative is in a strong position to do some initial bargaining with the nonpar bank. Before arranging to clear the nonpar checks through the par bank in town, the representative of Bank A may call on the nonpar bank and point out that Bank A incurs costs in handling the nonpar checks while the nonpar bank benefits from the exchange revenue. Because of these benefits to the nonpar bank, the representative may suggest that "in fairness" perhaps the nonpar bank would like to place a new or larger compensating balance with Bank A. Although the issue may be presented in terms of fairness, the nonpar bank generally realizes the wisdom of placing such a compensating balance with Bank A because Bank A has the option of arranging to present the nonpar checks through its par competitor. The value of the nonpar bank's compensating balance with Bank A reduces Bank A's cost below the original X dollars.

When there are a par and nonpar bank in the same town, therefore, Bank A can improve its position by tacitly playing one bank against the other. Bank A can try to obtain a better compensating balance from the nonpar bank or from the par bank, but in either case it improves its position at the expense of the nonpar bank.

The nonpar bank in a town with a par competitor may be subjected to further pressure. Other large banks, through their correspondent networks, also receive checks drawn on the nonpar bank. Each of these city correspondents can negotiate with the nonpar bank and the par bank in town, using the same bargaining technique as that used by Bank A. The nonpar bank, if it is to act efficiently, cannot keep large compensating balances with each of the city correspondent banks. This implies that some of the correspondent banks develop relationships with the par bank in town, and thus the par bank receives credit for some of the exchange revenue that otherwise would go to its nonpar competitor.

Thus, in towns with a nonpar bank and a par bank not only the city correspondent bank but also the par bank is able to improve its position at the expense of the nonpar bank. In this situation a nonpar bank has increased incentive to become par, because it is being forced to maintain larger correspondent balances and because its par competitor is benefiting from exchange charges previously obtained by the nonpar bank.

Given the conditions of nonpar banking, this theoretical example suggests how, in a town with both a par and a nonpar bank, the various parties may act to improve their relative positions—usually at the expense of the nonpar bank. In practice, such situations are known to exist.[4] However, it appears that certain codes of propriety temper their fullest development.

Another reason why a nonpar bank may become par arises from the fact that out-of-town checks drawn on it are returned to the town through the competing bank. Both the bank and its customers may dislike this procedure, since certain customers who have established a relationship with one of the two banks may resent the competing bank's knowledge of their out-of-town financial transactions.

Of the 132 banks changing from nonpar to par during 1960–64, 16 (12 per cent) had been competing with a nonpar facility for some time before making the decision to become par. (Occasionally the two or more nonpar banks in a community changed to par at about the same time.)

Fifty-seven of the 132 banks (43 per cent) were confronted by some form of local competition. The other 75 banks (57 per cent) were in one-bank towns.

At year-end 1964, 7 per cent of the nonpar banks in one-bank towns were in metropolitan areas. However, of the 75 banks that changed from nonpar to par while located in one-bank towns, 27 per cent were in metropolitan areas. This percentage is almost *four times* the percentage of such banks that remained nonpar, suggesting that nonpar banks cannot exist very long in metropolitan areas. Reasons for this conclusion are discussed in Chapter IX.

Fifty-five banks in rural one-bank towns changed from nonpar to par during 1960–64—about 42 per cent of the nonpar banks that changed in the same period. Yet 72 per cent of the nonpar banks at year-end 1964 were in rural one-bank towns, where nonpar banking is strongest—and slowest to change. Why did 55 nonpar banks in these towns decide to become par? Their officials must have concluded that such a change would serve the best interests of their institutions. How such decisions come to be made and the results of such decisions are analyzed in Chapters VIII and IX.

4. This statement is based on confidential interviews with officials of nonpar and par banks; cited hereafter as "confidential interviews."

FACTORS INCREASING THE NUMBER OF NONPAR BANKS

From 1960 through 1964, 25 nonpar banks were chartered by state authorities and then insured by the Federal Deposit Insurance Corporation. As seen in Table 20, these new nonpar banks were located in

Table 20. New state banks in nonpar states, classified by class of bank and by state (1960–64)

	Class of Bank				
State	Member of the Federal Reserve System	Insured Nonmember Par	Insured Nonmember Nonpar	Noninsured *	Total
Alabama	1	8	—	—	9
Arkansas	—	3	4	—	7
Florida	1	62	1	—	64
Georgia	—	14	5	8	27
Louisiana	—	13	4	—	17
Minnesota	1	11	8	1	21
Mississippi	—	1	—	—	1
Missouri	1	12	—	1	14
North Carolina	—	—	1	—	1
North Dakota	1	1	—	2	4
South Carolina	—	5	—	—	5
South Dakota	1	—	2	2	5
Tennessee	—	3	—	—	3
Texas	—	54	—	14	68
Total	6	187	25	28	246

* Many of these banks subsequently became insured by the Federal Deposit Insurance Corporation.

Source: Special tabulation prepared by the Federal Deposit Insurance Corporation, 1966.

seven of the 14 nonpar states, almost one-third of them in Minnesota.

In addition to showing where nonpar banks are being chartered, the table contains the following information useful for placing the nonpar issue in perspective. In each of the 14 nonpar states, newly chartered state banks have the option of charging exchange, yet only 11 per cent of the new insured banks chose to do so. Furthermore, most of the new nonpar banks are in five states: Arkansas, Georgia, Louisiana,

Minnesota, and South Dakota. Another important point is that only a small percentage of new state banks—in a minority of the nonpar states—decided to begin operations as nonpar institutions. That officers and directors of many new banks apparently consider and reject the opportunity to charge exchange suggests that this source of revenue is not as attractive as adherents of nonpar banking suppose. This fact is particularly striking because the officials of a newly chartered bank undoubtedly seek various sources of revenue to enable the new bank to begin earning profits for its shareholders.

The status of new nonpar banks is further outlined in Table 21, where the nonpar status of new banks is related to the structure of local competition. Of the 24 new *nonpar* banks tabulated there, 11 were located in one-bank towns and 11 in towns with an existing nonpar bank. Most of these new nonpar banks were in rural areas. Of the 41 new *par* banks, 10 were in one-bank towns or towns with a

Table 21. New insured state banks in selected nonpar states, classified by par status and by structure of local competition (1960–64) *

Structure of Local Competition	Number of Nonpar Banks	Number of Par Banks	Total
One-bank town			
Rural	5	2	7
Metropolitan	6 †	4	10
Competing nonpar bank in town			
Rural	10	4	14
Metropolitan	1	——	1
Competing par bank in town	2	31	33
Total	24	41	65

* These are six of the seven states in which insured nonpar banks were established during 1960–64 (Table 20). Florida has been excluded to reduce distortion by one state and because the new nonpar bank shortly became par.
† Each is in Minnesota.
Source: Special tabulation prepared by the Federal Deposit Insurance Corporation, 1966.

nonpar bank and 31 in towns with another par bank. These figures confirm earlier findings that nonpar banking is largely a rural phenomenon and almost entirely a function of the absence of par competition (Chapter IV).

During the years 1960–64, 11 par banks changed to nonpar.[5] This practice occurred principally in Minnesota, which accounted for seven of the 11 cases. Nine of the banks changing from par to nonpar were in rural one-bank towns or in rural towns where the only competitor was a nonpar bank. Each of these nine banks remained nonpar after the change. Of the other two banks changing from par to nonpar, one was located in a one-bank town in a metropolitan area, and the second faced par competition in the same town. Neither of these banks remained nonpar; each reverted to par. Again one finds that nonpar banking succeeds principally in rural communities where par competition is absent.

If exchange charges are an attractive source of revenue, one would expect more banks to try to obtain such revenue. By regulation, banks that are members of the Federal Reserve System cannot charge exchange on items presented to them by the Federal Reserve banks. During the years 1960–64, 55 state banks in nonpar states withdrew from the Federal Reserve System.[6] Of these 55 banks, which then had the option of using exchange charges as a source of additional revenue, only three became nonpar—all of them in Minnesota. Seventeen banks that withdrew from membership in the Federal Reserve System and that were located in rural one-bank towns elected to remain par institutions. Again one may assume that the officials of those banks acted in the best interests of their banks when they rejected the opportunity to obtain additional revenue from exchange charges. Once more it seems evident that this source of revenue is of debatable value to banks, even those located in rural one-bank towns.

During the five years being considered, 16 established nonpar banks became insured by the Federal Deposit Insurance Corporation. The number of *insured* nonpar banks therefore increased, but of course this did not affect the *total* number of nonpar banks, insured and noninsured. As noted in Chapter IV, there were 72 noninsured nonpar banks at year-end 1964.

SUMMARY OF CHANGES

The absence or presence of par competition is found to be a principal explanation of the changes in nonpar banks from 1960 through

5. The information in this paragraph is from a special tabulation prepared by the Federal Deposit Insurance Corporation, Washington, 1966.
6. *Ibid.*

65

1964. There was a greater percentage decline in the number of nonpar banks in states permitting some form of branch banking, because of absorptions of nonpar banks and because of the introduction of par branches in towns that had previously been served principally by nonpar banks. Of 24 newly chartered nonpar banks, 22 were in towns lacking any par competition. Of the 11 banks changing from par to nonpar during the period, the nine that remained nonpar were in rural towns without a par competitor. Few banks, however, remain nonpar in towns where they are confronted by par competition.

During this same period, 55 banks in rural one-bank towns changed from nonpar to par. Factors that lead such banks to change are examined in Chapter IX, and these factors help explain other findings discussed in this chapter. In nonpar states many newly chartered state banks in rural one-bank towns choose not to begin operations as nonpar institutions, as do many state banks in nonpar states that withdraw from membership in the Federal Reserve System. Thus both groups voluntarily forgo an additional source of revenue.

VIII

A Case Study of Certain Banks Changing from Nonpar to Par: 1962-63

Excluding absorptions and conversions to national charters, 132 banks changed from nonpar to par during the five years from 1960 through 1964 (Table 19). Of these, 42 did so during 1962–63. Table 22 shows the structure of local competition confronting these 42 banks.

Table 22. Banks changing from nonpar to par, classified by structure of local competition (1962–63)

Structure of Local Competition	Number of Banks	Percentage
New par facility in town	14	33
Had competed with par facility in town	5	12
Had competed with nonpar facility in town	4	10
One-bank town		
Metropolitan	3	7
Rural	16	38
Total	42	100

Source: Special tabulation prepared by the Federal Deposit Insurance Corporation, 1966.

The percentage distribution in the table is similar to that of the 132 banks that changed from nonpar to par during the years 1960–64. Thirty-three per cent of the banks changing from nonpar to par in the two-year period did so shortly after they were confronted by new par competition in the same town. Twenty-two per cent of these banks were located in towns with established competing banks, par or nonpar. This confirms the fact, noted in the preceding chapter, that the

67

presence of a competing bank in town frequently stimulates a nonpar bank to change to par.

SELECTION OF A SAMPLE GROUP OF BANKS

While 62 per cent of the banks changing from nonpar to par during 1962–63 either faced local competition or were located in metropolitan areas, the other 38 per cent (16 banks) were in rural one-bank towns. Even without the stimulus of local competition, the officials of these 16 banks apparently decided that a change from nonpar to par would be advantageous to their institutions despite the loss of a known source of revenue—exchange charges. Their decision is particularly significant because 72 per cent of the nonpar banks at year-end 1964 were also located in rural one-bank towns.

In contrast to banks changing from nonpar to par in towns with new or established competition or in growing metropolitan areas, the economic environment of these 16 banks in rural one-bank towns is assumed to be more stable through time. Therefore measures of operating performance before and after the change should reflect more clearly the policies of each of these banks than would be the case for banks facing new or changing competition.

To analyze the reasons why the 16 banks changed from nonpar to par, certain measures of operating performance will be examined *before* and *after* the years of change.[1] For an evaluation of possible changes in their operating performance a standard of comparison is needed. The 16 banks were in eight nonpar states. In the same eight states there were 409 nonpar banks in rural one-bank towns at year-end 1964. These banks were also nonpar in 1961, although data are available for only 404 of them. The 409 banks serve as the *control group* and thus provide a standard with which to compare the performance of the 16 banks that changed from nonpar to par during 1962–63.

1. The objective of this case study is to examine the operating characteristics of certain banks *before* and *after* their change from nonpar to par. Operating ratios for 1961 are the earliest available, and ratios for 1964 are the latest available from the bank supervisory agencies in Washington. Therefore this study is limited to banks that changed from nonpar to par in the two intervening years, 1962–63. This lack of data currently precludes analysis of operations in the years following 1964. Such further analysis is desirable because the banks that changed may have been still in a period of transition in 1964.

FINDINGS OF THE CASE STUDY

For the 16 banks that changed from nonpar to par and for the control group of 409 banks that remained nonpar, Table 23 shows the mean operating ratios in the years 1961 and 1964.[2] Here one sees that in 1961 each of the mean operating ratios is very similar for both groups. This finding is what one would expect, because in 1961 both groups of banks consisted of nonpar institutions in rural one-bank towns in the same nonpar states.

Since during the years 1962–63 the 16 banks changed from nonpar to par, the mean operating ratios in 1964 are for a group of 16 *par* banks in rural one-bank towns and 409 *nonpar* banks in rural one-bank towns in the same nonpar states. Comparing the 16 banks with the 409 banks in 1964 yields statistically significant differences in only two of the ratios. Considering profitability as measured by *Net current earnings/Total capital accounts*, the 16 banks had significantly higher profitability than did the 409 banks that remained nonpar. The other ratio in which the two groups of banks are significantly different is *All other revenue/Total operating revenue*. As would be expected, this ratio, which reflects the revenue from exchange charges, is significantly less for the 16 banks that became par.

These findings suggest a paradox. The 16 banks that changed from nonpar to par gave up exchange charges as a source of revenue, yet they became more profitable. Further examination of the table provides a possible explanation.

The ratios for the 409 nonpar banks show little change between 1961 and 1964. There is little difference in their sources of revenue in 1964 as compared with 1961. Similarly, the only minor difference in their asset structure is that the percentage of net loans to total assets increased about four points while the percentage of cash to total assets decreased about four points.

Certain of the ratios for the 16 banks, however, show major changes. Average profitability, as measured by *Net current earnings/Total capital accounts*, increased from 14.8 to 17.2 per cent, and, as noted, the figure of 17.2 is significantly greater than the mean figure of 14.4 per cent for the 409 banks. Assuming that there was no decline in "Total capital accounts" between 1961 and 1964 for the 16 banks,

2. In this case study the operating ratios and the test for statistical significance are the same as those described in Chapter V.

Table 23. Mean operating ratios of certain banks that changed from nonpar to par during 1962–63 and a control group of 409 similar banks that remained nonpar (1961, 1964)

Operating Ratio	1961		1964	
	Nonpar	Nonpar	Par	Nonpar
A. Profitability				
1. Net current earnings				
Total assets	1.4	1.5	1.6	1.5
2. Net current earnings				
Total capital accounts	14.8	13.5	**17.2**	**14.4**
B. Sources of revenue				
1. Interest and dividends on government securities				
Total operating revenue	26.2	23.5	21.5	23.5
2. Interest and dividends on other securities				
Total operating revenue	5.9	5.9	5.6	5.9
3. Revenue on loans				
Total operating revenue	53.7	56.0	63.3	57.6
4. Service charges on deposit accounts				
Total operating revenue	4.9	3.7	4.9	3.4
5. All other revenue				
Total operating revenue	9.4	10.9	**4.7**	**9.5**
C. Asset structure				
1. Government securities				
Total assets	33.0	29.9	28.3	28.8
2. Other securities				
Total assets	9.9	10.5	8.9	10.7
3. Loans (net)				
Total assets	33.7	37.2	45.5	41.7
4. Cash assets				
Total assets	22.3	21.5	16.0	17.8
Total number of banks	16	404	16	409

Note: Figures in boldface are those that are significantly different, based on the two-sample T-test.

the increased profitability must be due to greater "Net current earnings," which in turn is explained by greater revenue and/or lower expenses. Although the selected operating ratios do not include any expense ratios, it is reasonable to assume that total operating expenses did not decrease from 1961 through 1964 but actually increased somewhat. These assumptions lead one to conclude that the increased profitability of the 16 banks that changed from nonpar to par during the years 1962–63 was due to an increase in various sources of revenue more than sufficient to offset the loss of exchange revenue.

In interpreting Table 23, a word of caution is necessary. The sources of revenue are outlined by five component operating ratios, the sum of which must account for 100 per cent of total operating revenue. If the amount of exchange revenue decreases, the fifth ratio (*All other revenue/Total operating revenue*) must decrease, assuming that the loss of exchange revenue is not more than offset by increases in other miscellaneous revenue reported in the item "All other revenue." Thus, given a decrease in the fifth ratio, the sum of the other four ratios must increase so that the sum of the five operating ratios continues to account for 100 per cent of the total operating revenue.

Recognizing this statistical phenomenon, for those banks that changed from nonpar to par and thereby gave up exchange as a source of revenue, one might expect a decrease in the fifth ratio and small increases in each of the other four ratios. This expectation, however, is based on the assumption that bank policies did not change markedly except for the decision to become par. If those policies did change and were reflected in changes in the various sources of revenue, then one would expect a decrease in the fifth ratio and various changes in the other four ratios.

The information in the table suggests that various policies of the 16 banks did in fact change when the banks changed from nonpar to par. Their revenue on loans became more important—increasing about 10 points, from 53.7 to 63.3 per cent of total operating revenue. At the same time, revenue from government securities made a smaller contribution to total operating revenue than it had in 1961. This relationship is confirmed by changes in the asset structures of the banks. Net loans increased from 33.7 to 45.5 per cent of total assets, while holdings of government securities decreased from 33.0 to 28.3 per cent.

Two other related findings are also set forth in Table 23. First, the 16 banks that changed from nonpar to par apparently did not attempt to offset the loss of exchange revenue by increasing the service charges on deposit accounts, since such service charges accounted for 4.9 per cent of total operating revenue in both 1961 and 1964. Second, the ratio of *Cash assets/Total assets* decreased from 22.3 per cent in 1961 to 16.0 per cent in 1964. "Cash assets" in the numerator of this ratio represent principally balances with correspondent banks. While these 16 banks thus reduced their correspondent balances and increased their earning assets, the 409 banks that remained nonpar similarly economized on their correspondent balances.

IMPLICATIONS OF THE CASE STUDY

This case study of 16 banks that changed from nonpar to par answers certain questions but raises some others.

The fact that these banks operated more profitably after becoming par—notwithstanding the loss of exchange revenue—suggests that they were not operating as efficiently as possible before their decision to change from nonpar to par. For example, the increased importance of loans as a source of revenue implies that these banks, before the change, had not been fully meeting the loan demands of their trade areas. This is a tentative finding, based on the experience of only 16 banks; as noted, the loan ratios for the banks that changed are not significantly different from the ratios of those that remained nonpar.

If the 16 banks were not operating as efficiently as possible before their decision to become par institutions, why did not their officers make policy adjustments necessary for greater efficiency and profitability—and *also* retain exchange charges as a source of revenue? Such a procedure undoubtedly exists in some nonpar banks that maximize profits both by efficient operation and by exchange charges. That the officers considered and rejected this option suggests that they saw possible advantages in the management of a par institution that would outweigh the loss of exchange income. Why officials of nonpar banks might thus voluntarily give up exchange revenue without the stimulus of new competition in the same town is considered in Chapter IX.

IX

Some Economic Consequences
of Nonpar Banking

Certain characteristics of nonpar banks may be now summarized:

1. Nonpar banks generally are small institutions located in rural one-bank towns (Chapter IV). However, as will be pointed out in this chapter, the exceptions to this generalization are important.

2. Using certain measures of operating performance, one finds that in only several characteristics do nonpar banks differ significantly from similar par banks in nonpar states (Chapter V).

3. In most nonpar states there exist par nonmember banks that are as profitable—and in some cases more profitable—than similar nonpar banks.

4. The two groups of banks achieve comparable profitability by means of a slightly different "mix" of components in their total operating revenue. Compared with similar par banks, nonpar banks rely more on exchange charges as a source of revenue and less on service charges on deposit accounts.

5. Concerning investing and lending policies, statistically significant differences are seldom found between similar nonpar and par banks. However, nonpar banks maintain larger correspondent balances, on the average, than do similar par banks.

NONPAR BANK PRACTICES AND CUSTOMERS

The average small depositor of a nonpar bank does not understand what nonpar banking is, nor does he generally realize that the bank is nonpar.[1] To him his bank is the same as any other bank.

1. Information from confidential interviews.

When a depositor of a nonpar bank writes a check to a merchant or resident in the same town, the recipient of the check probably deposits it in the same bank—nonpar banking being usually a phenomenon of one-bank towns. In this case there is no exchange charge.

When a depositor of a nonpar bank writes a check to someone in the general trade area of his bank, there may be no exchange charge even though the check is deposited in a nearby bank rather than in the drawee bank.[2] The absence of an exchange charge in this case is explained by the fact that nonpar banks in a trade area may agree to honor checks drawn on each other at par.[3] Under such an agreement a check drawn on nonpar Bank A and deposited in nearby nonpar Bank B will be honored at par by Bank B. In turn Bank A (the drawee bank) will honor the item at par when it is presented for collection. Because of this agreement among nonpar banks in a trade area, many nonpar depositors and recipients of nonpar checks in the area are not affected by exchange charges. However, as will be shown in Chapter X, special par agreements contribute to the cost burden on correspondent banks that process these items.

It is when a nonpar check goes *outside* the town or general trade area that an exchange charge is made by a nonpar bank. In this case either the recipient of the check or a bank in the clearing process usually pays the exchange charge and considers this payment to be a cost of doing business. Thus, because the exchange charge is paid by an outsider, the small depositor of a nonpar bank may be unaware that his bank is nonpar.

While many nonpar bank depositors do not understand nonpar banking, others may—and they accept the situation for various reasons. First, the practice seldom affects the average small depositor because his checks are honored at par in his general trade area. Only checks sent to an outside individual or organization are honored at less than par, and the outsider rarely finds it practical to complain to a small depositor about the practice. Second, the practice may be customary throughout the trade area. A small depositor may realize that his bank is nonpar but may have no choice because it is the only bank in town and nearby banks may also be nonpar institutions. Third, a small depositor may accept his bank's reasons for the practice. A principal reason given by a nonpar bank is that an exchange charge is

2. The term "general trade area" in this context is necessarily vague. In practice the general trade area is often a county, but at times the area reflects economic relations rather than precise geographic designations.

3. Confidential interviews.

a legitimate shipping fee for transferring settlement funds to a distant recipient of a check.

A large depositor of a nonpar bank frequently is treated differently than a small depositor. A large local depositor—an automobile dealer, a farm equipment distributor, or the owner of a grocery store—often sends numerous checks, many of sizable amounts, to major corporations. Since corporations selling to such local merchants would be confronted with considerable amounts of exchange charges if they accepted nonpar checks, they often require payment in par funds, sometimes as a condition of the sales contract. Faced with such a requirement, the local merchant has two alternatives: He can open an account in a distant par bank, or he can request the nonpar bank to honor his checks at par. Not wishing to lose the account to a par bank, the nonpar bank usually agrees to honor all or some of the depositor's checks at par. The checks of this depositor are then printed or stamped to indicate that they are collectible at par.[4] As a result of this bilateral agreement the major outside seller is paid in par funds. Under the circumstances each of the three parties generally finds the arrangement to be satisfactory. However, as will be explained in Chapter X, such arrangements contribute to the cost burden on other banks that must process these special items.

In addition to many major corporations, other recipients of checks insist on par funds. The United States government requires payment at par on checks payable to it or its various agencies. Ironically, many states that authorize nonpar banking also have laws requiring that checks payable to the state and its agencies must be paid at par. Such states include Mississippi and North Carolina.[5]

North Dakota is unique in having a state-owned bank, the Bank of North Dakota. A state statute requires that any collection item payable to the state or its subdivisions and sent by the Bank of North Dakota to any state bank or banking association in North Dakota must be paid at par.[6] Not to comply with this requirement is to be guilty of a misdemeanor.

Concerning nonpar checks, one finds that recipients with economic or legislative power are often able to enforce payment at par. Less powerful and less sophisticated recipients generally pay exchange charges.

4. Confidential interviews.
5. Mississippi, *Mississippi Code, Annotated* (1956), c. 2, sec. 5220. North Carolina, *General Statutes* (1963), c. 53, sec. 73.
6. North Dakota, *Century Code, Annotated* (1959), c. 6–09, sec. 13.

THE EXTENT OF ABSORPTION OF EXCHANGE CHARGES

Absorption of exchange charges has been considered in Chapter III but principally in terms of the interagency controversy about the practice. A recent survey conducted in 10 nonpar states by the Federal Deposit Insurance Corporation provides information for examining the current practice of absorbing exchange charges.[7]

At times a depositor of a nonpar bank may receive a check drawn on a distant nonpar bank. In such a case the depositor's nonpar bank has the choice of either collecting this exchange charge from the depositor or absorbing the charge itself. Collecting this exchange charge may make the depositor aware of the practice of nonpar banking; absorbing it is a cost for the bank.

To discover the general policy adopted by nonpar banks confronted with such a choice, the nonmember banks in the survey were asked whether, in the majority of cases, they collected exchange charges on nonpar items deposited by customers. The responses to this survey question are tabulated in Table 24.

Of the *nonpar* banks in the survey, 61 per cent collect exchange charges from depositors, and 39 per cent do not. (This fact need not contradict the earlier statement that many small depositors do not understand the practice of nonpar banking, because these depositors only rarely receive checks drawn on distant nonpar banks.) The percentages are exactly the same for the nonmember *par* banks: 61 per cent collect charges, and 39 per cent do not. Thus in the 10 nonpar states covered by the survey a similar percentage of nonpar and par nonmember banks collect exchange charges from their depositors.

As discussed in Chapter III, the controversy about absorption of exchange charges has centered on the practice of actively absorbing such charges as a method of competing for correspondent balances. Because of the 1943 ruling by the Board of Governors of the Federal Reserve System (as qualified by the $2 Rule), only nonmember banks may legally absorb exchange charges.

To learn the extent of absorption of exchange charges by correspondent banks, the nonmember banks in the special survey were asked if, in the majority of cases, they cleared checks drawn on other

7. For details of the survey procedure, see Chapter VI. The questionnaire used in the survey is reproduced in Exhibit A–1 of the Appendix.

nonpar institutions through correspondent banks that absorbed exchange charges (Exhibit A–1).

In five of the 10 nonpar states covered by the survey, there was no reported clearing of nonpar items through correspondent banks that

Table 24. Policies of nonmember banks in ten nonpar states concerning collection of exchange charges on nonpar items deposited by customers (1966) *

Geographic Categories	Collect Exchange Charges on Deposits of Nonpar Items		Do Not Collect Exchange Charges on Deposits of Nonpar Items	
	Percentage of Nonpar Banks	Percentage of Par Banks	Percentage of Nonpar Banks	Percentage of Par Banks
Five nonpar states where *no* absorption was reported by correspondents	67	63	33	37
Five nonpar states where absorption was reported by correspondents	51	60	49	40
Total (10 nonpar states)	61	61	39	39

* This table is constructed from replies to question 4(a) of the "Survey of Par Clearance": "When the customers of this bank deposit nonpar items drawn on other banks, does this bank, in the majority of cases, collect the exchange charges on such nonpar items from the depositing customer?"

As described in the text and outlined in Table A–8 of the Statistical Appendix, the survey provides a 25 per cent sample of nonmember banks in the 10 states.

Source: Special tabulation prepared by the Federal Deposit Insurance Corporation, 1966.

absorb exchange charges. In these five states—Arkansas, Minnesota, North Dakota, South Dakota, and Tennessee [8]—nonpar banks and par banks are similar in their policies concerning collection of exchange charges from customers who deposit nonpar items drawn on other institutions. Sixty-seven per cent of the surveyed nonpar banks and 63 per cent of the surveyed par banks make such collections (Table 24).

8. Special tabulation prepared by the Federal Deposit Insurance Corporation, Washington, 1966.

In the other five states included in the special survey—Alabama, Florida, Georgia, Mississippi, and Missouri—the practice of clearing nonpar items through correspondent banks that absorb exchange charges was reported. In these states it is principally the nonpar banks that clear nonpar items through such correspondent banks. Forty-seven per cent of the nonpar banks in the survey reported these clearing arrangements, as against only 16 per cent of the par banks.[9] In the five states where absorption by correspondent banks was reported, nonpar banks tend to differ from par banks in their policies concerning collection of exchange charges from customers who deposit nonpar items drawn on other institutions. Fifty-one per cent of the surveyed nonpar banks and 60 per cent of the surveyed par banks make such collections (Table 24).[10]

In states where nonpar items are cleared through correspondent banks that absorb exchange charges, a nonpar bank is confronted by two sets of choices concerning its processing of nonpar items drawn on other banks. These sets of choices are presented schematically as follows:

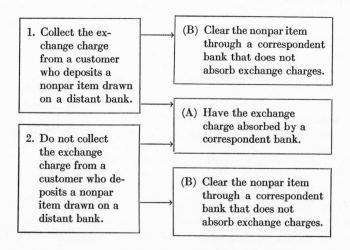

The general effects of these choices on the profits of a nonpar bank may be summarized as follows:

9. This statement is based on Table 25.
10. The difference may have arisen as a fluctuation of random sampling.

Case 1(B) Collect the exchange charge from the depositor.
           No effect on the profits of the nonpar bank.*
Case 1(A) Collect the exchange charge from the depositor.
           Profits of the nonpar bank are higher.†
Case 2(A) Do not collect the exchange charge from the depositor.
           No effect on the profits of the nonpar bank.*†
Case 2(B) Do not collect the exchange charge from the depositor.
           Profits of the nonpar bank are lower.

Having developed this conceptual framework for the sets of choices, it is desirable to examine actual bank practices. The answers to questions 4(a) and 4(b) of the "Survey of Par Clearance" (Exhibit A–1) provide the necessary information, and these answers are tabulated in Table 25.

For both groups of banks the most common practice is to collect the exchange charge from a customer who deposits a nonpar item and then clear this item through a correspondent bank that *does not* absorb exchange charges [Case 1(B)]. However, 55 per cent of the par banks follow this policy in contrast to only 30 per cent of the nonpar banks. Disregarding handling costs, this policy leaves the level of profits the same because the bank of deposit is basically acting as a collecting agent for a distant nonpar bank.

In contrast to the nonmember par banks, more nonpar banks clear distant nonpar items through correspondent banks that absorb exchange charges. Forty-seven per cent of the nonpar banks have such clearing arrangements. But although 21 per cent of the nonpar banks have such clearing arrangements and *also* have the policy of collecting such exchange charges from their depositors [Case 1(A)], only 5 per cent of the par banks follow a similar set of practices. Twenty-six per cent of the nonpar banks do not collect exchange charges from depositors but clear such items through correspondent banks that absorb exchange charges [Case 2(A)]. This figure of 26 per cent for the nonpar banks contrasts with the 11 per cent of par banks that report a similar set of practices.

The preceding findings present for the first time some measures of the extent of absorption of exchange charges. In contrast to nonmember par banks in the same states, nonpar banks are *less* likely to collect exchange charges from customers who deposit nonpar checks and

---

* Disregarding the handling costs.
† Disregarding the opportunity cost of maintaining a correspondent balance sufficient to warrant the correspondent bank's absorbing the exchange charge.

Table 25. Policies of nonmember banks in five nonpar states concerning absorption of exchange charges (1966) *

Sets of Choices †	Nonpar		Par	
	Number of Banks	Per-centage	Number of Banks	Per-centage
Case 1(B) Collect from depositor. Do not have absorbed.	38	30	99	55
Case 1(A) Collect from depositor. Have absorbed.	26	21	9	5
Case 2(A) Do not collect from depositor. Have absorbed.	33	26	19	11
Case 2(B) Do not collect from depositor. Do not have absorbed.	28	23 ‡	52	29
Total	125	100	179	100

* This table is constructed from replies to the "Survey of Par Clearance," which provides a 25 per cent sample of nonmember banks in selected nonpar states. The five states included in the table are Alabama, Florida, Georgia, Mississippi, and Missouri.

† These sets of choices are further explained in the text.

‡ Figure increased to next round number so that the sum of the column is 100.

Source: Special tabulation prepared by the Federal Deposit Insurance Corporation, 1966.

more likely to clear such items through correspondent banks that absorb exchange charges.

It is not clear, however, whether nonpar banks are less likely to collect exchange charges because they can have them absorbed or whether nonpar banks are more likely to have exchange charges absorbed because they prefer not to collect them from their customers. While the direction of causation is not evident from these data, Table 24 indicates that in the five states where there was no reported absorption by correspondent banks, 67 per cent of the nonpar banks collect exchange charges from their depositors, in contrast to the figure of 51 per cent for the nonpar banks in the other five states. Such a relationship suggests that in the five states where there is absorption by correspondent banks nonpar banks are less likely to collect exchange charges from customers because they can arrange to have the charges absorbed by correspondent banks. This analysis implies that if absorption of exchange charges were completely prohibited, nonpar banks would not be impelled to become par. Many nonpar banks might adjust by beginning to collect exchange charges from customers who deposit nonpar items drawn on distant banks.

WHY SOME NONPAR BANKS BECOME PAR:

A GENERAL EXPLANATION [11]

As discussed in Chapter VII, the principal reason why nonpar banks become par is the introduction of a competing par facility in the same town. While the spur of competition explains much, it is also found that banks in rural one-bank towns occasionally change from nonpar to par (Chapters VII and VIII). The analysis in the preceding sections suggests why nonpar banking gradually decreases, even in rural one-bank towns.

A changing trade area contributes to a decline in nonpar banking, and such changes occur most frequently in rural communities close to expanding metropolitan areas. In the first place, agreements by banks to par each other's checks become less practical in a trade area where new banks are being chartered and ownership of existing banks is likely to change. In some cases new bank management may have little sympathy with nonpar banking and even oppose the practice. A second reason is that long-time residents of the area may become more mobile as access to the city improves, and they may occasionally find their nonpar checks questioned or discounted in other trade areas. Such situations make more depositors aware of nonpar banking because they are confronted with the cost and inconvenience of the practice. In the third place, new residents of the area may come from places where par banking is the accepted practice. These new residents may accept nonpar banking if it does not directly affect them, but they are unlikely to tolerate it in situations where their nonpar checks are questioned or discounted. Many of these new residents may

11. The ideas for this section were developed and tested in confidential interviews with bankers. Particularly instructive were comments made by officials of banks that had recently changed from nonpar to par.

commute to the metropolitan area, where they have the option of opening an account with a par bank.

Another major factor contributing to a decline in nonpar banking is the increasing number of special par arrangements required of a nonpar bank by its larger depositors. Such arrangements—made, as already explained, to obtain the accounts of new industries entering the community—have several important results for a nonpar bank. (1) The growing number of these par arrangements and the increasing number of attendant special items entail additional processing work for the nonpar bank. (2) By agreeing to par the checks of its large depositors, the nonpar bank is sacrificing its best source of exchange revenue: those accounts that frequently send many sizable checks outside the general trade area. (3) It becomes generally known in the community that the nonpar bank is making par arrangements with some large depositors. Other customers who become aware of these arrangements may not be directly affected, but they may be somewhat resentful because various customers are being treated differently by the bank.

In addition to the changing trade area and the increasing complexities imposed by special par arrangements, other factors contribute to a decline in nonpar banking.

New management may at times change a nonpar bank to par. The former management may have continued its established nonpar policy without evaluating the effects of such a policy on the bank. The new management, often trained in methods of par banking, may evaluate the broad implications of a nonpar policy and decide that the institution should become par. Such a change in policy by one bank is likely to affect gradually the policies of remaining nonpar banks in the area.

In competing for new industrial accounts a nonpar bank may find itself at a disadvantage. It can offer to make special par arrangements, and often these are acceptable to potential large depositors. However, some corporations reject such arrangements because of a general corporate policy or because they regard the arrangements as a possible nuisance. A large corporation that has a plant in a community with a nonpar bank has the practical option of maintaining its account with a par bank in a major city.

By reexamining its nonpar policy, the officers of a nonpar bank may consider both the actual costs and the opportunity costs of maintaining that policy. In addition to possible customer displeasure, the additional handling required for special par arrangements, and the possibility of losing potential industrial accounts, the reexamination may indicate that the bank is maintaining excessive correspondent balances in order to have exchange charges absorbed. By becoming par, the bank would be better able to justify the collection of such charges from depositors and then clear the items through the most efficient correspondent networks.

Spreading metropolitan areas, new industry in small towns, and reexamination of policies concerning absorption of exchange charges are phenomena more prevalent in the nonpar states of the South than in those of the upper Middle West. The preceding analysis explains why changes from nonpar to par by banks in rural one-bank towns have been almost entirely limited to southern nonpar states (Table 19).

THE BROAD IMPACT OF NONPAR BANKING

The theory and practice of nonpar banking is that exchange charges should be paid by individuals and corporations located outside the general trade area of the nonpar bank. This means that exchange charges are paid by residents in other parts of the nonpar state and by residents of other states. That the practice of nonpar banking affects interstate commerce is not accidental; it is intentional.

In contrast to some large suppliers who insist on payment in par funds, businesses that receive nonpar checks of small amounts often accept the practice and pay the exchange charges as a cost of doing business. From their point of view, insisting on payment in par funds is not worth the cost and inconvenience involved. Confronted by this operating expense, a business will try to compensate for it by charging its customers slightly higher prices—the customers who pay with par checks as well as those who pay with nonpar checks. All of them pay slightly more than they would if every check were collectible at par.

A regulated public utility in a nonpar state provides an excellent model of the shifting economic incidence imposed by nonpar banking. In a simplified version, the argument is very precise. The state utility commission permits the regulated public utility a certain rate of return on its investment, but the utility's expenses must be acceptable to the commission. Given the utility's investment base, its level of expenses, and its permitted rate of return, a structure of rates is established. Because a utility in a nonpar state must pay some exchange charges, its level of expenses is higher than it would be if there were no such exchange charges. Given the same investment base and the same permitted rate of return, this higher level of expenses implies a higher structure of rates. These rates apply to all the utility's customers, those who pay with par checks and those who pay with nonpar checks.[12]

The preceding analysis, which demonstrates that nonpar banking results in a shifting of costs among various groups of individuals, raises questions of social equity. Should customers of utilities in nonpar states be required to pay higher rates because a certain group of banks maintains a nonpar policy? Should residents of other states be required to pay slightly higher prices for many goods and services because certain states permit nonpar banking? These questions of social equity should be recognized as such and discussed in terms of desired social policy.

In addition, the practice of nonpar banking should be analyzed concerning its economic efficiency. If, by necessity, nonpar banking imposes a cost burden on other individuals and corporations, here is a powerful argument for eliminating the practice—unless there are compelling social or political reasons for its continuation. Even so, if the procedure of nonpar banking is economically inefficient, then there is a strong case for developing a procedure to remove the cost burden of nonpar banking and *subsidize directly* the nonpar banks. Chapter X presents such an analysis of the cost burden of nonpar banking.

A MODEL NONPAR BANK BENEFITING

FROM EXCHANGE CHARGES

Two conditions are necessary for a bank to achieve maximum benefits from a nonpar policy. First, it should be as efficient as possible in all areas of its banking operations. Second, it should receive a high, and preferably increasing, level of revenue from exchange charges while at the same time having a low, and preferably decreasing, level of costs in maintaining its nonpar policy. For purposes of analysis, the first condition is assumed to be fulfilled.

The second condition is likely to occur when a bank is the only nonpar bank (or one of few nonpar banks) in a generally par area that is experiencing rapid growth. Such a bank is able to obtain an increasing number of depositors, many of whom send checks outside the bank's community. In this way the nonpar bank achieves a high and growing level of revenue from exchange charges. Because the checks drawn on this nonpar bank are sent to various recipients and

12. While all customers must pay slightly higher rates for their utility service, the majority of customers probably pays with par checks, so the greater share of the incidence falls on this group of customers.

are deposited in diverse banks, the impact of its nonpar policy is broadly diffused and therefore unlikely to generate a strong response from many individuals and corporations, each of which receives only a small number of the checks drawn on the nonpar bank. Because this nonpar bank is located in a predominantly par area, most of the checks received by its depositors are drawn on par banks. Therefore it need not collect many exchange charges from its customers, and it may prefer to absorb such charges rather than make some of its customers aware of the cost and inconvenience of nonpar banking.

This statement of the second condition may be outlined graphically as follows:

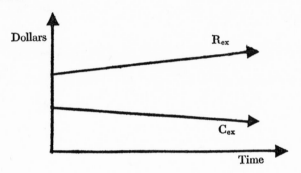

R_{ex} = Dollar revenue from exchange charges through time.
C_{ex} = Dollar cost of absorbing exchange charges for customers through time.

From the graph one notes that the difference between R_{ex} and C_{ex} increases through time. For the nonpar bank in such a situation, this means that its net income from exchange charges is increasing through time.

In practice the model nonpar bank is likely to be located in an expanding metropolitan area (or on its fringe) where most of the other banks are par. Furthermore, since this is likely to be a growing residential community, the bank obtains many individual depositors without having to solicit large commercial accounts that may require special par arrangements.

The special survey conducted by the Federal Deposit Insurance Corporation provides some important data with which to test this model.[13] As shown in Table A–4 of the Statistical Appendix, Minnesota has 34 nonpar banks located in metropolitan one-bank towns. Eight of

13. For details of the survey procedure, see Chapter VI. The questionnaire used in the survey is reproduced in Exhibit A–1 of the Appendix.

these banks were included in the special survey of 25 per cent of the nonmember banks in Minnesota. Accounting for *8 per cent* of the nonpar banks surveyed in Minnesota, these eight banks in metropolitan one-bank towns accounted for *31 per cent* of the total exchange revenue reported by all the nonpar banks surveyed in Minnesota.[14] Ninety-two per cent of the nonpar banks were in rural areas and accounted for 69 per cent of the aggregate reported revenue from exchange charges. When analyzing the cost burden of nonpar banking, discussed in Chapter X, one must recognize that a disproportionate share of nonpar items is generated by a small number of nonpar banks in suburban areas of nonpar states.[15]

The description of the model states that a nonpar bank in a generally par area may prefer to absorb exchange charges on nonpar items deposited by its customers. Two reasons are given for such a policy: (1) The number of such items is likely to be few, and (2) the nonpar bank may prefer to absorb the charges rather than make some of its customers aware of the disadvantages of nonpar banking. While the data are limited, of the eight nonpar banks in metropolitan one-bank towns surveyed in Minnesota, five (62.5 per cent) reported that they did not collect exchange charges on nonpar items deposited by their customers.[16] Of the 104 surveyed banks in rural areas of the state, only 22 per cent reported a similar policy of not collecting exchange charges on deposits of nonpar items.[17]

In the comparative ratio analysis of Chapter V, it is found that the income reported under item 1(e) of the "Report of Income and Dividends" provides a significantly greater percentage of total operating revenue for the 79 nonpar banks in metropolitan one-bank towns (12.0) than it does for the control group of nonpar banks in rural one-bank towns (9.3).[18] This relationship fits the model nonpar bank benefiting from exchange charges.

14. Special tabulation prepared by the Federal Deposit Insurance Corporation, Washington, 1966.

15. It is likely that, on the average, nonpar banks in suburban areas are larger in deposit size than those of rural areas. Therefore part of the greater volume of nonpar checks is associated with the difference in deposit size. Recognizing this relationship does not detract from the important finding that much of the cost burden on other banks is being imposed by a small number of nonpar banks.

16. Special tabulation prepared by the Federal Deposit Insurance Corporation, Washington, 1966.

17. *Ibid.*

18. As specified in Chapter VI, item 1(e) of the "Report of Income and Dividends" is a composite item. The complete description is "Other service charges, commissions, fees, and collection and exchange charges." Exchange charges are the principal component of item 1(e), as explained in Chapter VI.

Table 26. Mean operating ratios of eight nonpar banks in metropolitan one-bank towns in Minnesota (1964)

Operating Ratio	Eight Surveyed Nonpar Banks in Metropolitan One-Bank Towns in Minnesota *	79 Nonpar Banks in Metropolitan One-Bank Towns †	306 Nonpar Banks in Rural One-Bank Towns in Minnesota ‡
All other revenue **			
Total operating revenue	15.7	12.0	10.5
Service charges on deposit accounts			
Total operating revenue	6.4	5.1	3.5
Net current earnings			
Total assets	1.1	1.3	1.0
Net current earnings			
Total capital accounts	15.1	14.0	11.0

* These figures are from a special tabulation prepared by the Federal Deposit Insurance Corporation, 1966.

  † From Table 12.

  ‡ From Table 11.

  ** Included in this category is income from various commissions and fees. As noted in Chapter VI, the major component is income from exchange charges.

As another test of the model nonpar bank, Table 26 summarizes some selected operating measures of the surveyed nonpar banks in metropolitan one-bank towns in Minnesota and provides some standards for comparison. Compared with the two other groups of banks, the selected eight banks reported greater percentages of their total operating revenue coming from item 1(e) *and* from service charges on deposit accounts. The eight banks are also seen to be generally more profitable, particularly when measured in terms of return on capital accounts. These findings, which fit well the model nonpar bank benefiting from exchange charges, indicate that exchange charges contribute more to the total operating revenue of certain suburban banks in Minnesota than they do to the revenue of many small banks in rural areas of the state.

SUMMARY

While the theory of nonpar banking is understood by few individuals, in practice its impact falls on many different groups of people in diverse ways.

The Theory and Practice of Nonpar Banking

When a nonpar bank makes a special par arrangement with a large depositor, the accounts of other depositors continue to be processed on a nonpar basis and so are receiving differential treatment. Usually a special par arrangement is made with a large depositor who is required to pay major suppliers in par funds. Such an arrangement may also be offered to attract the account of a large new industry entering the nonpar bank's community. These par arrangements may satisfy the parties involved, but, as will be shown in Chapter X, they place an additional cost burden on other banks.

Recent information from a special survey by the Federal Deposit Insurance Corporation reveals that absorption of exchange charges by correspondent banks is basically a regional phenomenon. No evidence of this practice is found in the nonpar states of the upper Middle West. In those states where it does exist, nonpar banks more often have such clearing arrangements than do nonmember par banks. Furthermore, where they are able to have exchange charges absorbed by a correspondent bank, fewer nonpar banks collect exchange charges on deposited nonpar items than do nonmember par banks in the same states.

When nonpar banks in rural one-bank towns decide to become par, the factors contributing to this decision include the expansion of metropolitan areas and the establishment of new industries in communities with nonpar banks. These conditions are more often found in the southern nonpar states than in the nonpar states of the upper Middle West. Their relative absence in the upper Middle West, together with prohibitions on branch banking and the strong custom of nonpar banking, suggest that the practice of nonpar banking will be slow to change in that region.

The impact of nonpar banking is broad. It results in higher prices for various residents and nonresidents of nonpar states. Furthermore, the incidence of these higher prices is greater among purchasers who pay with par checks than among those who pay with nonpar checks. This shifting of costs poses questions of social equity.

X

The Cost Burden
of Nonpar Banking

The principle of nonpar banking is that an exchange charge should be paid by a recipient located outside the nonpar bank's local trade area. Because exchange charges are thus paid by outsiders, it is necessary to examine nonpar banking in the broader context of the nation's commerce, particularly the nation's banking system.

In 1964, nonpar banks received an estimated $15,000,000 to $16,000,000 in revenue from exchange charges (Chapter VI). Although certain costs were incurred in obtaining this exchange revenue, clearly the nonpar banks—10 per cent of the nation's banks located in 14 states—benefit from the practice. It is appropriate to consider whether this practice imposes a cost burden on the great majority of the nation's banks.

Historically nonpar banks justified an exchange charge as a fee paid by a distant recipient of a check for the service of transferring settlement funds to his bank (Chapter II). However, the practice of transferring funds in the nation's banking system has changed considerably. Today it is seldom necessary to settle the clearing of checks by means of a physical transfer of funds. Rather, the clearing of checks is usually settled by means of bookkeeping transactions among banks. These transactions are principally made at local clearinghouses, through correspondent balances, or through reserves maintained with the Federal Reserve banks. But while modern clearing systems have eliminated the original justification for exchange charges, the practice continues, mainly because of custom and because such exchange charges provide a comfortable source of revenue for nonpar banks.

NONPAR BANKING NECESSARILY IMPOSES ADDITIONAL

COSTS ON THE BANKING SYSTEM

Costly special clearing arrangements are necessary for nonpar checks. With minor exceptions, checks drawn on nonpar banks cannot be cleared through the Federal Reserve System (Chapter II). For this reason many banks must use special sorting and handling procedures to keep separate the nonpar checks that they process for customers. Such nonpar checks must be cleared at all stages through the correspondent banking system.

The general process of clearing a nonpar check through the correspondent banking system may be diagramed as follows:

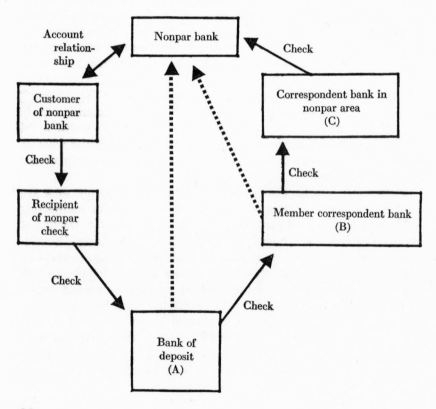

If the recipient of the check deposits it in the nonpar bank, there is no exchange charge, since exchange charges apply only to checks going outside the local trade area of the nonpar bank.

At times the bank of deposit, Bank A, sends the nonpar check directly to the nonpar bank. This usually occurs if Bank A is itself a principal correspondent bank in a nonpar area—for example, in Georgia or Minnesota. In such a case the practice of nonpar banking, permitted only in some states, affects banks within the nonpar states.

Although Bank A and Bank B may be located in par states, they are affected by the practice of nonpar banking, which is permitted only in some states. This is the interesting case, and the one selected for principal consideration in the subsequent empirical analysis of the cost burden of nonpar banking.

Nonpar checks also require special handling because someone must pay the exchange charges. Theoretically, and usually in practice, the recipient of a nonpar check pays the exchange charge. However, as pointed out in Chapter IX, the exchange charge is sometimes paid (absorbed) by the bank at which the recipient deposits the check or by another bank in the clearing process.

Because of a ruling by the Board of Governors of the Federal Reserve System, a member bank can absorb no more than two dollars in exchange charges per month for any one customer (Chapter III). To comply with this ruling, each member bank must record the exchange charges on all nonpar checks processed by it and then collect such charges from the recipients who deposited them at the bank. Many nonmember banks, although they need not comply with the $2 Rule believe that any exchange charge should be paid by the recipient of the nonpar check. This means they must record the exchange charges on all nonpar checks processed and in turn collect these charges from the customers who deposited the checks. Thus, in order to pass exchange charges back to the recipients of nonpar checks, a bank must keep record of (1) all the nonpar checks it receives, (2) the persons depositing or cashing these checks, and (3) the amount of exchange involved for each nonpar check.

If a bank absorbs an exchange charge rather than collecting it from the recipient of the check, this absorption is a cost to the bank. Given the decision to absorb an exchange charge, conceivably there are two principal alternatives: (1) If the bank is to maintain the same level of profits, the cost of absorption must be offset by means of additional revenue obtained from the bank's other customers, who are therefore subsidizing the absorption of exchange charges for a certain group of depositors. (2) If the cost of absorption is not offset, the result must be reduced profits for the bank's shareholders. An exception to this occurs when collecting an exchange charge from a customer costs the bank more than absorbing the charge. In such a case, clearly the cost to the banking system exceeds the benefit to the nonpar bank.

There is a third possibility. Some banks, rather than passing exchange charges back to depositors or absorbing such charges themselves, have the exchange charges absorbed by a correspondent bank. Because of the Federal Reserve ruling, only nonmember banks can legally absorb many exchange charges, and some have in fact developed sizable correspondent balances by doing so.[1] However, no bank provides such a service for nothing. If a nonmember correspondent bank is to incur the cost of absorbing exchange charges for another bank, then it generally requires that a correspondent balance be maintained with it and that the value of such a balance offset—or more than offset—the cost of absorbing exchange charges. Some bankers see an apparent advantage in having exchange charges absorbed by a correspondent bank. What they fail to recognize is that they must pay for this service, usually by maintaining larger nonearning correspondent balances or by receiving less of other services in return for the same correspondent balances.

In accordance with the Federal Reserve ruling, most exchange charges are passed back to depositors of nonpar checks. There are three principal procedures by which this can be done; each involves additional handling costs:

First, in the process of accepting deposits, tellers may watch for nonpar checks and charge the customer at the time of deposit. This procedure requires that tellers remember the names of nearby nonpar banks and take time to check through the various items in a deposit and collect appropriate exchange charges. Although the cost of this procedure is limited to the time and effort expended by the tellers, it is practical only when a moderate number of nonpar items are deposited and can be readily remembered or identified.

Second, a deposit may be accepted and credited to the depositor's account at par, subject to the bank's ability to collect all the funds on the deposited items. When a deposit is thus accepted at par on a conditional basis, subsequent steps are necessary to pass back any exchange charges to the customer who presented nonpar items. These

1. This statement is based on confidential interviews with officials of the Federal Deposit Insurance Corporation.

steps may be summarized as follows: (1) Sort all checks to find those drawn on nonpar banks. (2) Identify the customer who deposited (or cashed) such items. (3) Calculate the appropriate amount of exchange charges to be collected from the customer. (4) Advise the customer of the nonpar items in his deposit and charge him by billing him directly or debiting his account. (5) Maintain records of these billings. The costs of taking these steps are *additional* to the costs that would be involved if all checks were collectible at par.

Third, a deposit may be accepted at par on a conditional basis, but the bank, instead of billing the customer for exchange charges shortly after the deposit, may cumulate such charges and bill the customer for them periodically. The additional steps involved in this procedure are basically the same as those outlined for the second procedure, except that the bank may be able to reduce the costs of preparing advices and billing customers on a daily basis. In practice many banks follow the second procedure for customers who deposit only an occasional nonpar item and the third procedure for those who deposit many nonpar items. Confronted with additional handling costs for nonpar checks, banks try to make arrangements to minimize these costs.

Other factors also add to the cost burden of processing nonpar items. For example, exchange rates vary among nonpar states and occasionally among nonpar banks within a state. These variations require additional time for sorting, billing, and record keeping.

Then, too, as discussed in Chapter IX, a nonpar bank may agree to honor at par checks drawn by certain of its customers. The checks of these customers are usually printed or stamped to indicate that they are payable at par. In sorting procedures these par checks of nonpar banks must be identified. At times par items are not immediately recognized, and in such cases a depositor may be billed for an inappropriate exchange charge, which subsequently must be refunded.

Occasionally a nonpar bank agrees to honor checks drawn on it at par if they are presented by a certain correspondent bank.[2] Thus, in order to obtain par funds, other banks often route checks drawn on such a nonpar bank through the correspondent bank that has the par agreement. This situation requires that various correspondent banks keep informed of such bilateral par agreements, and results in checks being cleared by circuitous routes.

All these variations contribute to time lags in the clearing of nonpar checks, which in turn mean slower collection of funds. Also they may

2. Confidential interviews.

delay the notification of a recipient of a nonpar check that is uncollectible due to insufficient funds or an order to stop payment.

The lack of standardization in the clearing of nonpar checks leads to an increase in the number of errors, not only because of the additional steps required for processing nonpar items but because of such variations as nonstandardized schedules of exchange rates, par checks on nonpar banks, and special par agreements among banks.

The occasional nonpar item, received by an individual or business not acquainted with the practice, can be particularly costly for other banks. A person aware of exchange charges may dislike them but accept them. A person unaware of exchange charges is confronted by a new situation when his bank collects from him the exchange charge on a check that he had assumed to be par. Unhappy about this unexpected charge, the depositor is likely to question an officer of his bank about it. The officer must take time to explain that the charge is made by the nonpar bank on which the check was drawn and is being passed back to the recipient of the check.

Having considered why the practice of nonpar banking necessarily imposes a cost burden on other banks, it is desirable to try to measure this cost burden and its relation to the benefits received by nonpar banks.

RESULTS OF A SPECIAL SURVEY USED TO MEASURE THE

COST BURDEN OF NONPAR BANKING

To measure the cost burden of nonpar banking on other banks, a special survey was conducted. A brief questionnaire was sent to the 37 largest banks in the nation, as measured by total deposits as of December 31, 1965. Table 27 shows their location.

The reasons for selecting these banks are as follows:

1. The selection, based on the criterion of deposit size, is objective.

2. The banks are located in par states, with the exception of the two banks in Texas.

3. They are all major correspondent banks, and process nonpar items for many of their country correspondents.

4. They accounted for about 35 per cent of total bank deposits in the United States as of December 31, 1965.

5. Use of a small sample avoids the double counting that would be involved if, for example, a larger sample were to include the major

banks in Atlanta and Minneapolis. A nonpar check sent from Georgia to Chicago is usually cleared through a major Chicago bank and also a major Atlanta bank.

6. In terms of the diagram on page 90, these 37 banks basically represent the case of Bank B (member correspondent bank), which receives many nonpar items from its smaller, outlying correspondent banks (A) and in turn sends these nonpar items to correspondent banks in nonpar areas (C).

A copy of the questionnaire used in this "Survey of Nonpar Clearance" is reproduced in Exhibit A-2. Replies were received from 33 of the 37 banks—a 90 per cent response. Twenty-nine of the replies were usable, and, unless otherwise noted, are the basis for the figures in the subsequent analysis.

Table 27. Location by state of the 37 largest banks in the United States, as measured by deposits on December 31, 1965

State	Number of Banks
New York	10
California	7
Pennsylvania	5
Illinois	4
Michigan	3
Ohio	2
Oregon	2
Texas	2
Massachusetts	1
Washington	1
Total	37

Source: Special tabulation prepared by the Federal Deposit Insurance Corporation, 1966.

The 29 banks, located almost entirely in *par states*, processed 14,200,000 nonpar items in 1965. (This figure should surprise those who view nonpar banking only as a historical phenomenon, practiced by some small banks in a few states.) Exchange charges on these 14,-200,000 nonpar items amounted to $1,472,000, of which $1,209,000 was passed back to customers and $263,000 absorbed or otherwise unrecovered by these banks. The average exchange charge was 10.4 cents per item.

In Chapter VI it was estimated that all the insured nonpar banks received a total of $15,000,000 to $16,000,000 in revenue from exchange charges during 1964. Thus the exchange charges of $1,472,000 on the nonpar items processed by the 29 large banks accounted for approximately 10 per cent of all exchange charges in 1964.

Of the total amount of exchange charges, $1,209,000 was passed back to the depositors of the nonpar checks. Processing the nonpar checks and obtaining the exchange charges from the customers cost the 29 banks $720,000, of which $457,000 were direct out-of-pocket costs (principally labor) and $263,000 were exchange charges absorbed or otherwise unrecovered by the banks. The direct costs of $720,000 amounted to 47 per cent of the benefits of $1,472,000 passed on to the nonpar banks.

Indirect costs were also involved in the processing of nonpar items by the 29 banks. To allocate indirect costs to the particular function of processing nonpar items is imprecise, and, as expected, the percentage allocation of indirect costs varied widely among the respondent banks. They reported a total of $236,000 in indirect costs of processing nonpar checks in 1965.

Thus for these 29 banks the total costs (direct plus indirect) of processing nonpar checks in 1965 amounted to $956,000. It must be emphasized that these are *additional* costs. The direct costs would not exist if all checks were cleared at par. Some indirect costs might continue to exist in the short run, but in the long run such factors as floor space, machine time, and supervision could be assigned to other functions within the bank.

Because most of the exchange charges on these checks were passed back to the recipients of the checks, in a sense the 29 banks incurred additional costs in their role as collection agents for the nonpar banks. The total cost burden of $956,000 is accounted for principally by the special handling required to process nonpar items and also, to a small extent, by the amount of exchange charges absorbed or otherwise unrecovered. In the latter case the 29 banks directly provided exchange revenue to the nonpar banks.

In this special survey the nonpar banks received $1,472,000 in revenue from the practice of charging exchange. To provide this revenue, the 29 banks incurred total additional costs of $956,000—or 65 per cent of the total benefits to the nonpar banks.

Because the banks in this special survey are located almost entirely in par states, nearly all the 14,200,000 nonpar items they processed during 1965 were sent to correspondent banks in the nonpar areas. These correspondent banks (represented by Bank C in the foregoing diagram) in turn had to process the items and send them to the nonpar banks on which they were drawn.

Certain of the principal correspondent banks in Georgia and Minnesota estimate that the processing of nonpar items costs them two to five cents per item *in addition* to what the cost would be if all checks cleared at par.[3] Given this range and assuming the average additional cost of processing nonpar items to be three cents per item, then the processing of the 14,200,000 nonpar items amounted to a total additional cost of $426,000 for the correspondent banks in the nonpar areas. Adding this figure of $426,000 (the estimated cost burden on the correspondent banks in the nonpar areas) to the previous estimate of $956,000 (the cost burden on the 29 banks in the survey) indicates a total cost burden of $1,382,000 for certain banks to provide exchange revenue of $1,472,000 to a group of nonpar banks.

Of the total exchange charges of $1,209,000 that these 29 banks billed to their customers, $485,000 was billed to 2,300 smaller correspondent banks, each of which also incurred additional costs in clearing the nonpar items. The $485,000 billed to them was about 40 per cent of the total of $1,209,000 in exchange charges billed by the 29 banks to their customers. As an approximation, therefore, it is estimated that the number of nonpar items processed by the 2,300 smaller banks was similarly about 40 per cent of the total of 14,200,000 nonpar items processed by the 29 banks. On this assumption the 2,300 smaller banks processed 5,700,000 nonpar items.

As a minimum, the additional cost per item for these smaller banks would be the figure of three cents per item used for the large correspondent banks in the nonpar areas. (For the 29 banks in the survey, the average total cost per item was 6.7 cents.) On this assumption the *minimum* cost burden for the 2,300 smaller banks was $171,000. Adding this minimum estimate to the preceding figure of $1,382,000 gives a total of $1,553,000. In terms of the diagram, this estimated total cost burden includes the additional costs incurred by those banks represented by A, B, and C.

Based on the preceding analysis, it is estimated that providing exchange revenue of $1,472,000 to a group of nonpar banks cost other banks *at least* $1,553,000. This is a minimum estimate of the cost burden. As will be explained shortly, the processing cost per item was greatest for those banks in the survey that processed the least number of nonpar items. In view of this relationship it is very probable that

3. This statement is based on confidential interviews with officials of various major correspondent banks in Atlanta, Minneapolis, and St. Paul.

the actual processing cost per item exceeded the figure of three cents used to develop the preceding minimum estimate of $171,000 for the 2,300 smaller banks. If the actual figure did exceed three cents per item, then the cost burden on other banks *further* exceeded the benefits of $1,472,000 in exchange revenue for the nonpar banks.

This analysis, demonstrating that in 1965 the cost burden on other banks exceeded the benefits to the nonpar banks, was based on about $1,500,000 of the estimated $15,000,000 to $16,000,000 in total exchange charges received by the nonpar banks during 1964. From a limited survey of 29 large banks one cannot estimate the total costs incurred by the nation's banks in providing this estimated total exchange revenue to the nonpar banks. However, the analysis shows how great the cost burden must be, because of the special procedures required for clearing and billing a nonpar item. Furthermore the additional cost of processing a nonpar item usually falls on several banks in the clearing process.

ECONOMIES OF SCALE IN PROCESSING NONPAR CHECKS

Table 28 shows the additional cost per item incurred by the 29 banks in their processing of nonpar checks as related to the number of nonpar checks processed by each bank. For the various categories in the table, both the mean and the median of the reported cost figures are presented. In most categories the mean and the median are close,

Table 28. Additional cost per item of processing nonpar checks, classified by number of nonpar items processed (figures in cents)

Number of Nonpar Items Processed	Additional Total Cost		Additional Direct Cost		Number of Banks
	Median	Mean	Median	Mean	
Under 50,000	19.3	22.8	12.4	16.1	8
50,000–100,000	7.9	7.5	7.4	6.6	3
100,000–200,000	10.0	10.2	7.2	7.9	4
200,000–500,000	7.7	8.8	6.4	7.1	5
500,000–1,000,000	6.1	6.1	5.0	5.0	2
1,000,000 and over	2.9	5.1	2.4	3.8	7

Source: Calculated from data provided by 29 banks responding to the "Survey of Nonpar Clearance," 1966.

although in some cases the mean exceeds the median because of the influence of extreme values.

The cost per item is substantially less for those banks processing large numbers of nonpar checks. This is true for both total additional cost and direct additional cost. For those banks processing more than 1,000,000 nonpar items in 1965 the median direct cost per item was 2.4 cents. For those banks processing fewer than 50,000 nonpar items the median direct cost per item was 12.4 cents. This finding suggests that banks which process large numbers of nonpar items are able to develop specialized procedures to reduce the direct cost per item. Furthermore the indirect cost per item is less for banks that are able to spread their allocation of indirect costs over large numbers of nonpar items. These findings indicate that there are economies of scale in processing nonpar items.

While economies of scale are possible, those banks that process smaller numbers of nonpar items are confronted by a substantial cost per item. Eight banks in this survey processed fewer than 50,000 nonpar items in 1965. For these banks the *median* direct cost per item was 12.4 cents and the median total cost per item 19.3 cents; the *mean* direct cost per item was 16.1 cents and the mean total cost per item 22.8 cents. Hence it is seen that the cost burden of nonpar banking falls more heavily on banks that process smaller numbers of nonpar items than it does on banks that process large numbers of nonpar items and are thus able to achieve economies of scale.

In addition to passing back exchange charges to other banks, the banks in this survey billed total exchange charges of $724,000 to corporate and individual accounts during 1965. To learn whether such charges were dispersed among many customers or concentrated among only a small number of corporate customers, each bank in the survey was asked to report the total exchange charges billed to the "accounts of the ten corporate customers which were billed the largest amounts for exchange charges during 1965" (Exhibit A–2). Twenty-six banks provided this information. Their 260 corporate customers were billed a total of $315,000 in exchange charges during 1965, and at least 6,000 other corporate and individual customers were billed $342,000 in exchange charges during the same year.[4] This relationship indicates that the practice of nonpar banking not only affects a small number of corporations to a great extent but also affects many corporations.

4. These figures are for 26 banks. The sum of $657,000 is necessarily less than the figure of $724,000, which is for 29 banks.

99

As is found to be the case for banks, it may be that corporations which receive many nonpar items are able to adjust to exchange charges as a cost of doing business more readily than can smaller businesses. While such a proposition is not tested in this study, it would seem to be valid in that a small corporation receiving occasional nonpar items may incur greater handling costs per item than a larger one, and also may be less able to include the cost of exchange charges in its pricing policy or to demand par funds from its customers.

The cost burden on other banks, then, is inherent in the practice of nonpar banking. If the practice of nonpar banking were to end, the cost burden on other banks would be removed. Such a consideration is further examined in the concluding chapter.

XI
Conclusions

Under present conditions there is no reason to expect a rapid end to the practice of nonpar banking. In 1917 the Federal Reserve Board stated that "in the near future checks upon practically all banks in the United States can be collected at par."[1] In studying the par collection controversy in 1929, Charles S. Tippetts concluded that "the procedure most advisable would be to let the matter rest as it is, leaving it to the passage of time to convert the exchange charging banks so that universal par remittance may become a reality."[2] Neither the expectation of rapid conversion nor the prediction of meaningful gradual change to par clearance has been confirmed. As noted in Chapter III, from 1942 through 1964 the total number of insured nonpar banks decreased by 940; but 360 were in three states that passed legislation *requiring* par clearance, 134 were in nine states where nonpar banking gradually came to an end, and 446 were in present nonpar states. Furthermore nonpar banking has declined most rapidly in states where statewide branching is prevalent. However, many of the present nonpar states specifically limit the extent of branch banking, notably Minnesota. There one finds the largest number of nonpar banks, and this number has *increased* in recent years.

Not only does the practice of nonpar banking impose a substantial cost burden on par banks, many of which are located outside the states permitting nonpar banking, but it has other debatable economic

1. *Third Annual Report of the Federal Reserve Board Covering Operations for the Year 1916*, p. 10.
2. Charles S. Tippetts, *State Banks and the Federal Reserve System* (New York, 1929), p. 332.

consequences. Although nonpar banks, given time, can adjust to the loss of exchange charges, many are reluctant to surrender this known source of revenue. There is no reason to expect a natural end to the practice in the foreseeable future. Therefore it is concluded that *legislation should be enacted requiring all banks to remit at par*— allowing a reasonable period of time for nonpar banks to adjust to the new situation.

While this legislation may be enacted at either the state or the national level, federal legislation is preferable for three reasons: (1) Although nonpar banks are state chartered, the practice of nonpar banking is *intended* to affect distant recipients of checks—many of whom are in other states.[3] (2) Whereas some states may pass legislation requiring par clearance, other states may not do so; therefore the cost burden will continue to exist, even though nonpar banks in only a few states will benefit from the practice. Also, because of the limited number of nonpar banks, other banks may be less able to achieve economies of scale in processing nonpar items. (3) Legislation at the national level may be more practicable, since attempts to pass par-clearance laws have been unsuccessful in some states (Chapter III).

A principal method by which nonpar banks can adjust to universal par clearance is through higher service charges on deposit accounts. The analysis in Chapter V indicates that this is the main difference in operating policies between nonpar banks and similar par banks. Since 88 per cent of the nonpar banks already have some service charges on deposit accounts, many of them can adapt to universal par clearance by simply adjusting their service-charge schedules without having to educate their customers to a new concept of banking operations. Another method of adjustment is suggested by the evidence presented in Chapters V, VIII, and IX. This evidence, although less strong, indicates that some nonpar banks may be able to reduce their correspondent balances and transfer some of these funds into earning assets.

By using extensive new data and by applying quantitative methods, this study analyzes the theory and practice of nonpar banking in the context of the nation's contemporary banking system. It is found that the privilege of charging exchange, granted to one group of banks,

3. This is an important distinction. The practice of charging exchange is intended to affect nonresidents of a state, whereas many other banking laws and practices of a state are intended principally to affect residents. Such laws and practices are concerned with questions of (1) whether to permit branch banking, (2) whether to permit noninsured banking or private banking, (3) whether to allow state banks to operate certain affiliates, such as insurance agencies.

102

imposes a major cost burden on other banks. Not only does the practice result in economic inefficiency, but it contributes to various social inequities. The current importance of exchange income for nonpar banks is analyzed, and it is found that—given time to adjust—nonpar banks can adapt to universal par clearance. However, because the practice of nonpar banking is unlikely to end rapidly and because a gradual ending is inefficient and inequitable, legislation is necessary to achieve universal par clearance. Such legislation should give nonpar banks time to adjust to the new situation.

Hopefully, the method of analysis and the information developed in this study will contribute to broader recognition of the issues of nonpar banking—and the resolution of a controversy that has continued for more than half a century.

Statistical Appendix

Table A–1. Number of nonmember
banks not on the par list, classified by
state (August 31, 1919)

State	Number of Banks
Alabama	209
Arizona	35
Arkansas	240
California	15
Colorado	64
Florida	139
Georgia	509
Illinois	117
Indiana	237
Iowa	208
Kansas	121
Kentucky	216
Louisiana	197
Maryland	5
Michigan	206
Minnesota	576
Mississippi	254
Missouri	325
Montana	45
Nebraska	350
New Mexico	11
North Carolina	409
North Dakota	304
Ohio	64
Oklahoma	136
Oregon	62
South Carolina	295
South Dakota	302
Tennessee	272
Texas	757
Virginia	206
Washington	54
West Virginia	123
Wisconsin	423
Wyoming	13
Total	7,499

Source: *Federal Reserve Bulletin,* V
(September 1, 1919), 888.

Table A–2. Insured nonpar banks, classified by state and by deposit size (December 31, 1964)

State	Deposit Size (millions of dollars)						Total Banks
	Under 1	1–2	2–5	5–10	10–25	25–50	
Alabama	5	21	38	11	1	—	76
Arkansas	12	31	39	8	3	—	93
Florida	2	5	22	6	—	—	35
Georgia	30	57	100	29	2	—	218
Louisiana	9	13	34	34	6	1	97
Minnesota	33	167	166	34	1	—	401
Mississippi	4	17	65	36	4	—	126
Missouri	5	12	21	7	—	—	45
North Carolina	—	13	29	5	4	—	51
North Dakota	7	27	54	8	—	—	96
South Carolina	4	13	21	—	2	—	40
South Dakota	10	47	41	5	—	—	103
Tennessee	7	28	21	8	2	—	66
Texas	11	9	6	—	—	—	26
Total	139	460	657	191	25	1	1,473
Percentage of 1,473	9	31	45	13	2	—	100

Source: Special tabulation prepared by the Federal Deposit Insurance Corporation, 1966.

Table A–3. Insured nonpar banks, classified by state and by population of community (December 31, 1964)

State	Population of Community								Total Banks
	Under 250	250– 499	500– 999	1,000– 2,499	2,500– 4,999	5,000– 9,999	10,000– 14,999	15,000– 49,999	
Alabama	1	5	21	29	16	2	2	—	76
Arkansas	8	8	32	31	9	4	1	—	93
Florida	—	—	7	16	4	7	1	—	35
Georgia	3	24	34	63	62	21	8	3	218
Louisiana	—	6	10	34	24	16	4	3	97
Minnesota	47	106	120	82	29	9	6	2	401
Mississippi	3	7	24	49	23	19	—	1	126
Missouri	3	11	11	13	4	3	—	—	45
North Carolina	2	8	17	22	2	—	—	—	51
North Dakota	11	21	27	35	2	—	—	—	96
South Carolina	1	5	7	18	6	3	—	—	40
South Dakota	14	35	30	21	3	—	—	—	103
Tennessee	6	18	14	18	4	5	1	—	66
Texas	2	6	14	3	1	—	—	—	26
Total	101	260	368	434	189	89	23	9	1,473
Percentage of 1,473	7	18	25	29	13	6	2	—	100

Source: Special tabulation prepared by the Federal Deposit Insurance Corporation, 1966.

Table A–4. Insured nonpar banks, classified by state and by structure of local competition (December 31, 1964)

State	One-Bank Town		Competing Nonpar Facility in Town		Competing Par Facility in Town		Total Banks
	Rural	Metro-politan	Rural	Metro-politan	Rural	Metro-politan	
Alabama	50	4	14	3	5	—	76
Arkansas	74	5	12	—	2	—	93
Florida	27	1	3	—	4	—	35
Georgia	114	5	84	2	12	1	218
Louisiana	49	5	32	—	10	1	97
Minnesota	308	34	39	2	16	2	401
Mississippi	70	6	37	—	13	—	126
Missouri	42	2	—	—	1	—	45
North Carolina	38	9	2	2	—	—	51
North Dakota	84	5	5	2	—	—	96
South Carolina	34	3	2	—	1	—	40
South Dakota	94	5	—	—	4	—	103
Tennessee	47	—	17	—	2	—	66
Texas	25	1	—	—	—	—	26
Total	1,056	85	247	11	70	4	1,473
Percentage of 1,473	77		18		5		100

Source: Special tabulation prepared by the Federal Deposit Insurance Corporation, 1966.

Table A-5. Percentage distribution by deposit size of nonmember banks in nonpar states (December 31, 1964)

Deposit Size (millions of dollars)	All Banks		Banks in Rural One-Bank Towns in Eight States *	
	Nonpar	Par	Nonpar	Par
Under 2	40	23	47	47
2–5	45	31	46	38
5 and over	15	46	7	15
Total	100	100	100	100

* Alabama, Arkansas, Florida, Missouri, North Carolina, South Carolina, Tennessee, and Texas.

Source: Special tabulation prepared by the Federal Deposit Insurance Corporation, 1966.

Table A–6. Schematic presentation of this study's analysis of comparative operating characteristics of nonpar and par nonmember banks (December 31, 1964)

State	Rural One-Bank Town Eight States Par	Rural One-Bank Town Eight States Nonpar	Six States	Competing Nonpar Facility in Town	Competing Par Facility in Town	Metropolitan One-Bank Town	Nonpar Banks Analyzed	Nonpar Banks Not Analyzed	Total Nonpar Banks
Alabama	18	50	—	14	5	4	73	3	76
Arkansas	21	73	—	9	2	5	89	4	93
Florida	28	27	—	3	4	1	35	—	35
Georgia	—	—	112	81	11	5	209	9	218
Louisiana	—	—	49	29	10	5	93	4	97
Minnesota	—	—	306	39	15	28	388	13	401
Mississippi	—	—	70	37	13	6	126	—	126
Missouri	208	42	—	—	1	2	45	—	45
North Carolina	12	38	—	2	—	9	49	2	51
North Dakota	—	—	84	4	1	5	93	3	96
South Carolina	10	34	—	2	1	3	40	—	40
South Dakota	—	—	91	—	4	5	100	3	103
Tennessee	64	47	—	17	2	—	66	—	66
Texas	170	24	—	—	—	1	25	1	26
Total	531	335	712	237	68	79	1,431	42	1,473
Percentage of Total Nonpar	—	23	48	16	5	5	97	3	100

Source: Special tabulation prepared by the Federal Deposit Insurance Corporation, 1966.

Table A–7. Revenue from "other service charges, commissions, fees, and collection and exchange charges" as a percentage of "total current operating revenue" of nonpar banks, classified by state (1964)

State	Percentage					Total Banks
	Under 5	5–10	10–15	15–20	20 and over	
Alabama	24	44	8	—	—	76
Arkansas	18	46	20	7	2	93
Florida	2	17	14	1	1	35
Georgia	22	118	63	12	3	218
Louisiana	24	58	9	3	2	96
Minnesota	37	188	121	37	18	401
Mississippi	18	82	20	5	1	126
Missouri	12	25	8	—	—	45
North Carolina	4	31	12	3	1	51
North Dakota	2	31	44	16	3	96
South Carolina	1	10	11	12	6	40
South Dakota	9	65	21	6	2	103
Tennessee	35	28	3	—	—	66
Texas	11	13	2	—	—	26
Total	219	756	356	102	39	1,472 *
Percentage of 1,472	15	51	24	7	3	100

* Excludes one bank having over $25,000,000 in deposits.
Source: Special tabulation prepared by the Federal Deposit Insurance Corporation, 1966.

Table A–8. Expected and actual coverage of the "Survey of Par Clearance," classified by the ten nonpar states included in this special survey (1966) *

State	Expected Coverage †		Actual Coverage	
	Nonpar	Par	Nonpar	Par
Alabama	19	18	13	17
Arkansas	23	16	20	17
Florida	9	46	7	42
Georgia	54	23	65	22
Minnesota	100	23	104	18
Mississippi	31	7	33	10
Missouri	12	103	7	88
North Dakota	24	5	26	6
South Dakota	26	3	18	2
Tennessee	16	35	20	38
Total Banks	314	279	313	260

* See Chapter VI for details about the "Survey of Par Clearance."

† These figures are approximately 25 per cent of the total banks in each category at year-end 1964. Because the survey was conducted over a three-month period, the actual number of banks surveyed should approximate these expected figures, allowing for differences due to sampling fluctuations.

Source: Special tabulation prepared by the Federal Deposit Insurance Corporation, 1966.

Table A–9. Net changes in insured nonpar banks, classified by state and by prevalent banking structure (1960–64)

Prevalent Banking Structure, by State *	Number of Insured Nonpar Banks		Net Change	
	December 31, 1959 †	December 31, 1964 ‡	Number	Percentage
Unit banking				
Arkansas	103	93	−10	−10
Florida	42	35	− 7	−17
Minnesota	391	401	+10	+ 3
Missouri	52	45	− 7	−13
North Dakota	96	96	——	——
South Dakota	101	103	+ 2	+ 2
Texas	31	26	− 5	−16
Total	816	799	−17	− 2
Limited branching				
Alabama	84	76	− 8	−10
Georgia	223	218	− 5	− 2
Louisiana	107	97	−10	− 9
Mississippi	137	126	−11	− 8
Tennessee	75	66	− 9	−12
Total	626	583	−43	− 7
Statewide branching				
North Carolina	81	51	−30	−37
South Carolina	61	40	−21	−34
Total	142	91	−51	−36
Total (all categories)	1,584	1,473	−111	− 7

* This classification is used by the Federal Deposit Insurance Corporation. See the *Annual Report of the Federal Deposit Insurance Corporation, 1964*, Table 50, p. 144.

† Excludes 15 nonpar banks in the following states: Alaska, Kansas, Oklahoma, Virginia, and West Virginia.

‡ Excludes two nonpar banks in Oklahoma.

Source: Special tabulation prepared by the Federal Deposit Insurance Corporation, 1966.

Appendix

SURVEY OF PAR CLEARANCE

Name of Bank:
City and State:
Certificate Number:
Date of Examination:

1. In this bank's Report of Income and Dividends for the calendar year 1965, how much of the amount reported for item 1(e) ("other service charges, commissions, fees, and collection and exchange charges") represents domestic remittance (exchange) charges against checks presented by mail for payment?
$ _____

2. In addition to such exchange income what other sources of revenue, if any, were important components of the amount reported in item 1(e) for the calendar year 1965?

	Source:	Amount:
(a)	_____	$ _____
(b)	_____	$ _____
(c)	_____	$ _____
(d)	_____	$ _____

3. As of December 31, 1965, which were this bank's three principal correspondent banks?

	Name	Location	Balance as of December 31, 1965
(a)	_____	_____	$ _____
(b)	_____	_____	$ _____
(c)	_____	_____	$ _____

4. When the customers of this bank deposit nonpar checks drawn on other banks:
   (a) Does this bank, in the majority of cases, collect the exchange charges of such nonpar items from the depositing customer?

   _____yes
   _____no

   (b) Does this bank, in the majority of cases, clear such nonpar items through correspondent banks which absorb the exchange charges?

   _____yes
   _____no

EXHIBIT A–2

SURVEY OF NONPAR CLEARANCE
(Selected Survey of the 37 Largest Banks)

Name of Bank:

1. The total number of nonpar items processed during 1965.

   _____

2. The total number of customer accounts billed for exchange charges during 1965.

   _____

   Please allocate this total figure between two broad categories.
   (a) Accounts of correspondent banks.

   _____

   (b) Accounts of corporate and individual customers.

   _____

3. The total exchange charges billed to customer accounts during 1965.

   $_____

   Please allocate these total exchange charges among three broad categories.
   (a) Accounts of correspondent banks.

   $_____

   (b) Accounts of the ten corporate customers which were billed the largest amounts for exchange charges during 1965.

   $_____

   (c) Accounts of all other corporate and individual customers.

   $_____

4. The processing of nonpar items involves steps additional to those which would still be necessary if all items were cleared at par. Please estimate the *additional* cost to your bank of processing nonpar items during 1965.
   (a) Direct out-of-pocket costs (such as labor and materials).

   $_____

   (b) Exchange charges against your bank which were absorbed by your bank or otherwise unrecovered.

   $_____

   (c) Allocation of indirect costs (such as floor space, machine time, and supervision).

   $_____

SUPPLEMENTARY STATEMENT FOR THE "SURVEY OF NONPAR CLEARANCE"
(Selected Survey of the 37 Largest Banks)

1. The answer to this question should indicate the extent to which nonpar checks (drawn on banks in certain states) are being processed by major banks in par states.

2. This question is intended to determine the number of customers who are *regularly* affected by nonpar items. These are the customer accounts which are billed for exchange charges nearly every month because the amount exceeds two dollars. This total figure may of course miss those bank customers who only deposit an occasional nonpar item and so are not billed for the exchange.

   If many nonpar items come from correspondent banks, this would indicate that the recipients of nonpar checks are diffused throughout the areas served by these city correspondents.

In interpreting these reported figures, it is recognized that several banks may be serving the same customer. However, there seems to be no practical method to eliminate such duplication.

3. The answers to this question should indicate the magnitude of exchange charges as they affect the customers of these 37 major banks.

Also the sum of the amounts reported here can be related to the total exchange revenue reported by all nonpar banks in 1965.

4. This question is very important to an analysis of the impact of nonpar banking. It has been argued that remittance (exchange) charges merely shift the cost of transferring funds from the drawer of the check to the recipient. However, it becomes evident that *additional* costs are involved because of the special clearing and billing procedures for nonpar items. The answers to this question will provide some measure of the additional costs involved in such special procedures.

The question has been divided into three parts. For maximum usefulness rather precise estimates are necessary for parts (a) and (b). Part (c) may have to be less precise, perhaps expressed in a reasonable range.

Bibliography

PUBLIC DOCUMENTS

Board of Governors of the Federal Reserve System. *Fifty-second Annual Report of the Board of Governors of the Federal Reserve System, Covering Operations for the Year 1965.* Washington, 1966.

Federal Deposit Insurance Corporation. *Annual Report of the Federal Deposit Insurance Corporation, 1964.* Washington, 1965.

———. "Assets, Liabilities, and Capital Accounts: Commercial and Mutual Savings Banks." Report of Call No. 72. Washington, 1965.

Federal Reserve Board. *Annual Report.* 1914–17.

U. S. Committee on Financial Institutions. *Report of the Committee on Financial Institutions to the President of the United States.* Washington, 1963.

U. S. House of Representatives, Committee on Banking and Currency. *Bank Holding Companies, Scope of Operations and Stock Ownership.* Eighty-eighth Congress, 1963.

———. *Hearings on H.R. 3956, Absorption of Exchange Charges.* Seventy-eighth Congress, Second Session, 1943–44.

U. S. Treasury Department, Comptroller of the Currency. *National Banks and the Future.* Report of the Advisory Committee on Banking to the Comptroller of the Currency. Washington, 1962.

BOOKS

Kent, Raymond P. *Money and Banking.* New York, 1966.

Miller, Melvin C. *The Par Check Collection and Absorption of Exchange Controversies.* Cambridge, Massachusetts, 1949.

Moody's Bank & Finance Manual. New York, April 1965.

Polk's Bank Directory. Nashville, 1959–65.

117

The Report of the Commission on Money and Credit. *Money and Credit: Their Influence on Jobs, Prices, and Growth.* Englewood Cliffs, New Jersey, 1961.

SPAHR, WALTER EARL. *The Clearing and Collection of Checks.* New York, 1926.

TIPPETTS, CHARLES S. *State Banks and the Federal Reserve System.* New York, 1929.

YULE, G. UDNY, and M. G. KENDALL. *An Introduction to the Theory of Statistics.* London, 1958.

ARTICLES AND PERIODICALS

Federal Reserve Bulletin. 1919–66.

KREPS, CLIFTON H., JR. "Characteristics of Nonpar Banks: A Case Study," *The Southern Economic Journal,* XXVI (July 1959), 44–49.

The New York Times. May 3, 1966.

"Nonpar Banking: Near the End of an Era?," *Monthly Review* (Federal Reserve Bank of Minneapolis), May 1966, 3–8.

VEST, GEORGE B. "The Par Collection System of the Federal Reserve Banks," *Federal Reserve Bulletin,* XXVI (February 1940), 89–96.

WYATT, WALTER. "The Par Clearance Controversy," *Virginia Law Review,* XXX (June 1944), 361–97.

STATUTES

Iowa. *Iowa Code, Annotated* (1949). c. 528, sec. 63.

Mississippi. *Mississippi Code, Annotated* (1956). c. 2, sec. 5220.

North Carolina. *General Statutes* (1963). c. 53, sec. 73.

North Dakota. *Century Code, Annotated* (1959). c. 6–09, sec. 13.

UNPUBLISHED MATERIAL

Board of Governors of the Federal Reserve System. "Member Bank Operating Ratios, Year 1964." FR 456 (Rev. 11–64). Washington.

Federal Deposit Insurance Corporation. "Report of Income and Dividends—Calendar Year 1964." Form 73. Washington.

JOHNSON, DAVID M. *The Nonpar and Exchange Charge Controversy Brought Up to Date.* The Stonier Graduate School of Banking, 1964.

OTHER SOURCES

Federal Deposit Insurance Corporation. Much of the data for this study was prepared as special tabulations by the Federal Deposit Insurance Corporation, Washington, 1965–66.

Interviews. Extensive confidential interviews with bank officials and bank supervisory authorities provided a principal source of information for this study. The bank officials were from various institutions: (1) nonpar banks in Georgia and Minnesota, (2) banks in Georgia that recently changed from nonpar to par, (3) large correspondent banks in Georgia and Minnesota, and (4) large correspondent banks in some par states.

Index

Absorption of exchange charges, 15, 20, 41, 82–83, 85, 91–92, 95–96; center of controversy, 15–17, 18; congressional hearings on, 17; cost of, 91–92; extent of, 76–81, 86, 88

Advisory Committee on Banking, 1962 report to the Comptroller of the Currency, 19–20

Bank holding companies, control of nonpar banks, 26–27

Bank of North Dakota, 75

Banking Act of 1933, 14, 15

Banking Act of 1935, 15–17, 21

Board of Governors of the Federal Reserve System, 20, 33; position concerning absorption of exchange charges, 15–17, 21, 76. See also Federal Reserve System; "Two-Dollar Rule"

Branch banking: branches of nonpar banks, 27–28, 59; impact on nonpar practice, 57–59, 60, 66, 101; nonpar branches of par banks, 28, 59; restrictions on, 88, 101

Checks, circuitous routing of, 7–8, 93

Commission on Money and Credit, 1961 report, 19

Committee on Financial Institutions, 1963 report to the President of the United States, 20

Common law doctrine concerning nonpar practice, 6, 10

Competition of par facility, impact on nonpar practice, 27, 28, 59–68 passim, 81

Comptroller of the Currency. See Advisory Committee on Banking

Correspondent balances maintained by nonpar banks, 38, 43–46 passim, 61–62, 72, 73, 82–83, 91–92, 102. See also Absorption of exchange charges

Correspondent banking: check clearing, 89–98 passim; theory of "par point," 60–62. See also Absorption of exchange charges; Correspondent balances maintained by nonpar banks

Exchange charge, 3, 6–7, 89; shifting of costs to consumers, 83–84, 88

Exchange draft, 7, 11

Federal Deposit Insurance Corporation, 20, 23, 30, 63, 65; position concerning absorption of exchange charges, 15–17, 21; 1942 study of nonpar banking, 17–18, 49, 51–52; 1966 "survey of par clearance," 52–53, 56, 76–79, 85, 88

Federal Reserve Act, 8–12 passim, 16, 18. See also Federal Reserve System

Federal Reserve banks: attempts to enforce par clearance, 10, 11–12, 14; check-clearing facilities, 8–10, 12, 65, 89. See also Federal Reserve System

Federal Reserve Board, 10, 12; power to issue rulings, 8–9; Regulation J, 9; statement concerning nonpar practice, 13, 101. See also Federal Reserve System

Federal Reserve System, 4, 8, 10–15 passim, 19, 20, 26, 30, 59, 90; withdrawals from membership, 14, 65, 66. See also Board of Governors of the Federal Reserve System; Federal Reserve Act; Federal Reserve banks, Federal Reserve Board; "Two-Dollar Rule"

Holding companies. See Bank holding companies

Kreps, Clifton H., Jr., 38n, 60n

National Monetary Commission, 4, 7–8
National and State Bankers Protective Association, 11
New York Times, The, editorial about nonpar banking, 20
Nonpar banking, practice defined, 3, 6–7
Nonpar states, term explained, 23

Operating ratios, 68n, 71; outlined and considered, 33–35

Panic of 1907, 7
Par list, 10, 12, 13, 28n
Par point, 60. See also Correspondent banking
Profitability of nonpar banks, 35–37, 41–45 passim, 69, 73, 87

Remittance charge. See Exchange charge

"Report of Income and Dividends," 34, 53, 86; description of item 1(e), 47

Service charges on deposit accounts, policy of nonpar banks, 37, 38–41, 43–46 passim, 71–72, 73, 87, 102
Special par arrangements of nonpar banks: with correspondent banks, 8, 93; with customers, 75, 81–82, 85, 88, 93; with other nonpar banks in the trade area, 74, 81
State legislation concerning nonpar banking: authorizing, 11–13; prohibiting, 19, 21, 101; proposed par clearance bills, 19, 20, 102; requiring par payment on certain items, 75
"Survey of Nonpar Clearance," 94–95

Tippetts, Charles S., statement about nonpar banking, 101
"Two-Dollar Rule," 18, 21, 76, 91

United States Congress, 4, 7, 11; hearings on absorption of exchange charges, 17; proposed amendment to the Federal Reserve Act, 18
United States government, requirements of payment at par on certain items, 75
United States Supreme Court, rulings on nonpar banking, 12